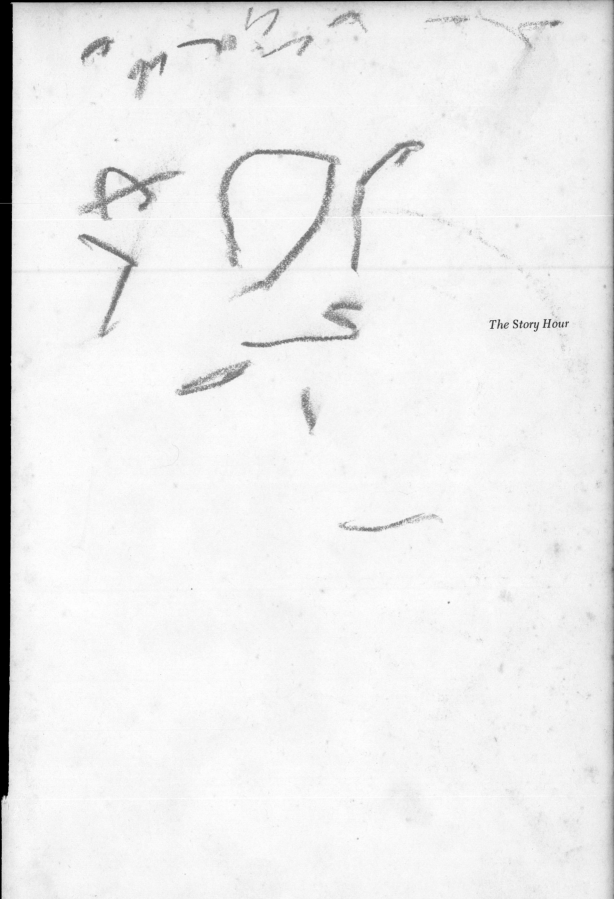

The Story Hour

Illustrations by

Franz Altschuler
George Armstrong
Robert Christiansen
Ralph Creasman
Helen Endres
John Faulkner
Seymour Fleishman
Robert Lostutter
Vernon McKissack
Carolynn Mazur
Eleanor Mill
Frank C. Murphy
Joseph Rogers
Dan Siculan
George Suyeoka
Donald G. Wheeler

The Story Hour

compiled by ESTHER M. BJOLAND

revised in consultation with ARLENE LABOW, *University of Chicago Nursery School*

Managing Editor ANNE NEIGOFF

STANDARD EDUCATIONAL CORPORATION

Chicago 1980

ACKNOWLEDGMENTS

We wish to express our deep thanks and appreciation to the following publishers, authors, and periodicals whose permission to use and reprint stories and poems has made this book possible.

JAMES T. BRADY
for "Mr. Groundhog Turns Around" and to *Jack and Jill Magazine* in which this story first appeared.

CHILDRENS PRESS, INC.
for *Six Foolish Fishermen* based on a folktale in Ashton's *Chap-books of the Eighteenth Century,* 1882, by Benjamin Elkin, copyright 1957; and for *Indian Two Feet and His Horse* by Margaret Friskey, copyright 1959 by Childrens Press, Inc.

COWARD-MCCANN, INC.
for "Gone Is Gone" from *Gone Is Gone* by Wanda Gág, copyright 1935 by Wanda Gág. Reprinted by permission of Coward-McCann, Inc.

DOUBLEDAY & CO., INC.
for "The White Goat" from *The Poppy Seed Cakes* by Margery Clark, copyright 1924; "The Play-house Key" and "The Ice-Cream Man" from *Taxis and Toadstools* by Rachel Field, copyright 1926; "Angus and the Ducks" from *Angus and the Ducks* by Marjorie Flack, copyright 1930; "A Fairy Went A-Marketing" from *Fairies and Chimneys* by Rose Fyleman, copyright 1918, 1920 by George H. Doran Company, reprinted by permission of Doubleday & Co., Inc., "Singing-Time" from *The Fairy Green* by Rose Fyleman, copyright 1923 by George H. Doran Company, reprinted by permission of Doubleday & Co., Inc.; and for "Mr. Apple Names the Children" from *Mr. Apple's Family* by Jean McDevitt, reprinted by permission of Doubleday & Co., Inc.

E. P. DUTTON & CO., INC.
for *Koala Bear Twins* by Inez Hogan, copyright 1955 by Inez Hogan. Condensed and reprinted by permission of E. P. Dutton & Co., Inc.

GOLDEN PRESS, INC.
for *The Color Kittens* by Margaret Wise Brown, copyright 1962 by Golden Press, Inc., reprinted by permission of Golden Press, Inc.

HARPER & BROTHERS
for "Park Play" from *I Live in the City* by James S. Tippett, copyright 1927 by Harper & Brothers.

LITTLE, BROWN & CO.
for "Morning" from *The Poems of Emily Dickinson* by Emily Dickinson; and for "The Umbrella Brigade" from *Tirra Lirra, Rhymes Old and New* by Laura E. Richards.

THE MACMILLAN COMPANY
for "The Little Turtle" from *Collected Poems* by Vachel Lindsay, copyright 1920 by The Macmillan Company, renewed 1948 by Elizabeth C. Lindsay, reprinted by permission of The Macmillan Company.

HERBERT R. MAYES
for "Holding Hands" by Lenore M. Link.

GRACE G. MITCHELL
for "Walking" by Grace Glaubitz.

THOMAS NELSON & SONS
for "Little Talk" from *That's Why* by Aileen Fisher, reprinted by permission of Thomas Nelson & Sons.

G. P. PUTNAM'S SONS
for "Hiding" and "The Sprinkler" from *Everything and Anything* by Dorothy Aldis, copyright 1925, 1926, 1927 by Dorothy Aldis, reprinted by permission of G. P. Putnam's Sons; "Somersault" from *All Together* by Dorothy Aldis, copyright 1925, 1926, 1927, 1928, 1934, 1939, 1952 by Dorothy Aldis, reprinted by permission of G. P. Putnam's Sons; and for "The Pancake" from *Tales from the Fjeld* by Peter Christian Asbjörnsen and Jörgen Moe, reprinted by permission of G. P. Putnam's Sons.

RAND MCNALLY & CO.
for "I Can Be a Tiger" by Mildred Leigh Anderson from *Child Life Magazine,* copyright 1938, 1966 by Rand McNally & Co.

WILLIAM R. SCOTT, INC.
for "Here Comes Daddy" from *Here Comes Daddy* by Winifred Milius, reprinted by permission of William R. Scott, Inc.

THE SOCIETY OF AUTHORS
for "A Fairy Went A-Marketing" and "Singing-Time" by Rose Fyleman, reprinted by permission of The Society of Authors as the literary representative of the estate of the late Rose Fyleman.

NANCY BYRD TURNER
for "The First Thanksgiving of All" by Nancy Byrd Turner.

ALBERT WHITMAN & CO.
for *What Mary Jo Shared* by Janice May Udry, illustrations by Eleanor Mill. Text copyright 1966 by Janice May Udry, illustrations copyright 1966 by Eleanor Mill, reprinted by permission of Albert Whitman & Co.

THE WORLD PUBLISHING CO.
for *Chie and the Sports Day* by Masako Matsuno, text copyright 1965 by Masako Matsuno, reprinted by permission of The World Publishing Co.

YALE UNIVERSITY PRESS
for "Neighbors" from *Songs for Parents* by James Farrar, reprinted by permission of Yale University Press.

Care has been taken to obtain permission to use copyright material. Any errors are unintentional and will be corrected in future printings if notice is sent to Standard Educational Corporation.

Art Direction and Design: Willis Proudfoot

Standard Book Number 87392-003-1

To
Boys and Girls
Everywhere

"When does the story hour come?" a little boy asked one day. "Show me on the clock."

The story hour is a magical hour. Sometimes you can show it on the clock, sometimes you cannot. Sometimes it comes just before you go to bed. Other times it may come on a rainy afternoon or on a sunny picnic day. Sometimes it even comes when you and your mother are walking down the street and she begins, "Pussy cat, pussy cat, where have you been?" or "Once there was a very young little dog whose name was Angus."

Whenever you say "Read me a story" or "Say a rhyme!" and your mother or father or perhaps your big sister says "Yes!"—that is the story hour. When you curl up in a chair and read a story or rhyme to yourself —that is the story hour, too!

And so we made *The Story Hour* book just for you. Here are all kinds of rhymes—Mother Goose rhymes, ABC rhymes, play-in-the-park rhymes, counting rhymes and rainy-day rhymes and rhymes about elephants and witches and fairies and spacemen!

Here are all kinds of stories, too—funny stories, magic stories, stories about little bears and kittens and goats. Here are stories about boys and girls—all kinds of boys and girls. A little Indian boy wants a horse—do you like horses, too? A little girl of Japan runs a funny kind of race. Mary Jo brings a surprise to Show and Tell Time. What do you bring?

When does the story hour come? It can come right now when you open this book and find stories to read and rhymes to say and wonderful, colorful pictures to see!

Here is *The Story Hour* book, just for you!

Contents

Time to Rhyme

Story Time

Time to Rhyme

SMILING girls, rosy boys,
  Come and buy my little toys;
Monkeys made of gingerbread,
And sugar horses painted red.

Rock-a-bye, baby, on the tree top!
When the wind blows, the cradle will rock,
When the bough breaks, the cradle will fall;
Down will come baby, cradle and all.

Dance, little baby, dance up high,
Never mind, baby, mother is by;
Crow and caper, caper and crow,
There, little baby, there you go.

Up to the ceiling, down to the ground,
Backwards and forwards, round and round;
Dance, little baby, and mother shall sing,
With the merry gay choral, ding, ding-a-ling.

Here's a ball for baby,
  Big and soft and round;
Here is baby's hammer,
  See how he can pound!
Here are baby's soldiers,
  Standing in a row;
This is baby's music,
  Clapping, clapping so!

Fishy, fishy in the brook,
  Daddy catch him on a hook,
Mommy fry him in a pan,
Johnny eat him like a man.

WHERE, oh, where has my little dog gone?
  Oh, where, oh, where can he be?
With his tail cut short and his ears cut long—
  Oh, where, oh, where can he be?

PUSSY CAT, pussy cat, where have you been?
  I've been to London to look at the Queen.
Pussy cat, pussy cat, what did you there?
I frightened a little mouse under her chair.

ONCE I saw a little bird
    Come hop, hop, hop;
So I cried, "Little bird,
    Will you stop, stop, stop?"
And went to the window
    To say "How do you do?"
But he shook his little tail
    And away he flew.

GOOD MORNING, Mrs. Hen.
    How many chickens have you got?
Madam, I've got ten.
    Four of them are yellow,
And four of them are brown,
    And two of them are speckled red,
The prettiest in town.
    Cluck! Cluck! Cluck! Cluck!

O VER in the meadow in the sand in the sun,
    Lived an old mother turtle and her little turtle one.
"Dig," said the mother.
"I dig," said the one.
So they dug all day in the sand in the sun.

Over in the meadow where the stream runs blue,
Lived an old mother fish and her little fishes two.
    "Swim," said the mother.
    "We swim," said the two.
So they swam all day where the stream runs blue.

Over in the meadow in a hole in a tree,
Lived an old mother owl and her little owls three.
   "Tu-whoo," said the mother.
   "Tu-whoo," said the three.
So they tu-whooed all day in the hole in the tree.

Over in the meadow by the old barn door,
Lived an old mother rat and her little rats four.
   "Gnaw," said the mother.
   "We gnaw," said the four.
So they gnawed all day by the old barn door.

Over in the meadow in a snug beehive,
Lived an old mother bee and her little bees five.
   "Buzz," said the mother.
   "We buzz," said the five.
So they buzzed all day in the snug beehive.

Bobby Shaftoe's gone to sea,
  Silver buckles on his knee;
He'll come back and marry me,
  Pretty Bobby Shaftoe!

Bobby Shaftoe's fat and fair,
Combing down his yellow hair;
He's my love forevermore,
  Pretty Bobby Shaftoe.

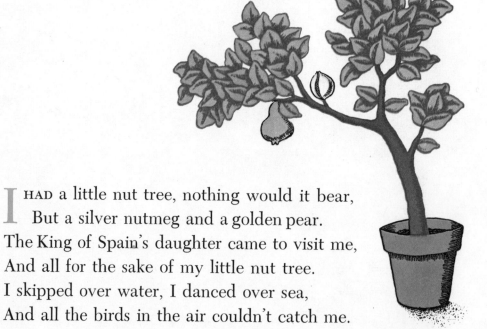

I had a little nut tree, nothing would it bear,
  But a silver nutmeg and a golden pear.
The King of Spain's daughter came to visit me,
And all for the sake of my little nut tree.
I skipped over water, I danced over sea,
And all the birds in the air couldn't catch me.

Spring is showery, flowery, bowery;
  Summer: hoppy, croppy, poppy;
Autumn: wheezy, sneezy, freezy;
  Winter: slippy, drippy, nippy.

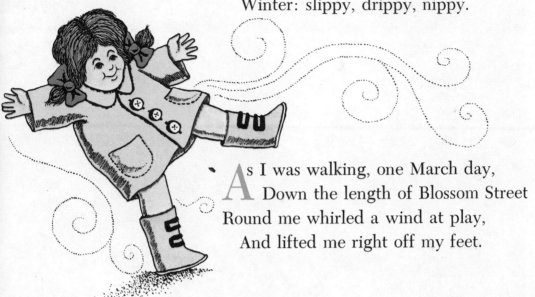

As I was walking, one March day,
  Down the length of Blossom Street
Round me whirled a wind at play,
  And lifted me right off my feet.

Ring a ring o'roses,
  A pocketful of posies.
Tisha! Tisha!
We all fall down.

THERE was an old woman tossed up in a basket,
    Nineteen times as high as the moon;
And where she was going, I couldn't but ask it,
    For in her hand she carried a broom.

"Old woman, old woman, old woman," said I,
    "O whither, O whither, O whither so high?"
"To sweep the cobwebs off the sky!"
    "Shall I go with you?" "Aye, by and by."

18

I ASKED my mother for fifty cents
  To see the elephant jump the fence.
He jumped so high
He reached the sky
And never came back 'till the Fourth of July.

19

SING a song of letters,
Making words is fun,
There's a word for everything
Underneath the sun.

There's a word for everything
We do and say and see,
And every word has letters
From our ABC.

A is an airplane I can fly,

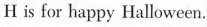

B is a blue ball bouncing by;

C is for circus, watch the clown!

D is for digging holes deep down.

E is an elephant I know,

F is for fun in frosty snow;

G is a goblin, gay and green,

H is for happy Halloween.

I is for ice cream, icy sweet,

J is for joyful jumping feet;

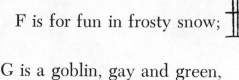

K is a kicking kangaroo,

L is for laughing and lonesome, too.

M is for muffins Mother makes,

N is for nibbling nuts and cakes;

O is an old owl, wise and fat,

P is a purring pussy cat.

Q is a queen, quite proud and shy,

R is a rocket roaring by;

S is my sister—she is small!

T is to tiptoe through the hall.

U is umbrella—up goes mine!

V is a lovely valentine;

W is for whistling, watch me blow,

X is in exit—and out we go!

Y is your yard where you can play,

Z is the zoo—we'll go some day!

RIDE away, ride away,
　　Johnny shall ride,
And he shall have pussy cat
　　Tied to one side;
And he shall have little dog
　　Tied to the other,
And Johnny shall ride
　　To see his grandmother.

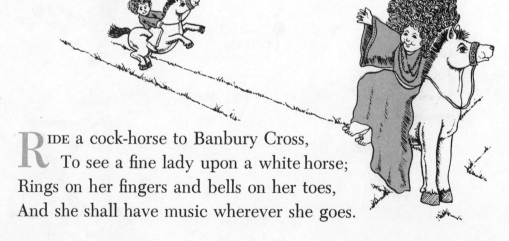

How many miles to Babylon?
　　Three score miles and ten.
Can I get there by candle-light?
　　Yes, and back again.
If your heels are nimble and light,
You can get there by candle-light.

RIDE a cock-horse to Banbury Cross,
　　To see a fine lady upon a white horse;
Rings on her fingers and bells on her toes,
And she shall have music wherever she goes.

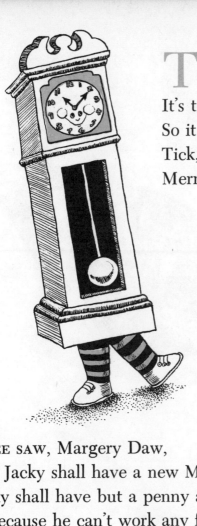

TICK, TOCK, tick, tock,
        Merrily sings the clock;
It's time for work, it's time for play,
So it sings throughout the day.
Tick, tock, tick, tock,
Merrily sings the clock.

SEE SAW, Margery Daw,
    Jacky shall have a new Master;
Jacky shall have but a penny a day,
    Because he can't work any faster.

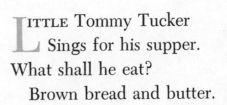

LITTLE Tommy Tucker
    Sings for his supper.
What shall he eat?
    Brown bread and butter.

THE Queen of Hearts,
  She made some tarts,
All on a summer's day.

The Knave of Hearts,
He stole the tarts,
  And took them clean away.

The King of Hearts
Called for the tarts,
  And beat the Knave full sore.

The Knave of Hearts
Brought back the tarts,
  And vowed he'd steal no more.

I saw a ship a-sailing,
  A-sailing on the sea;
And, oh! it was all laden
  With pretty things for thee!

There were comfits in the cabin,
  And apples in the hold;
The sails were made of silk,
  And the masts were all of gold.

The four-and-twenty sailors
  That stood between the decks,
Were four-and-twenty white mice
  With chains about their necks.

The captain was a duck,
  With a packet on his back;
And when the ship began to move,
  The captain said, "Quack! Quack!"

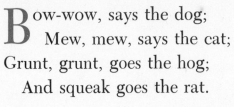

Bow-wow, says the dog;
    Mew, mew, says the cat;
Grunt, grunt, goes the hog;
    And squeak goes the rat.

Chirp, chirp, sings the sparrow;
    Caw, caw, says the crow;
Quack, quack, says the duck;
    And what cuckoos say, you know.

The north wind doth blow,
    We soon shall have snow,
And what will poor Robin do then?
    Poor thing!

He'll sit in a barn,
To keep himself warm,
And hide his head under his wing.
    Poor thing!

26

One misty, moisty morning,
  When cloudy was the weather,
There I met an old man
  Clothed all in leather.
He began to compliment
  And I began to grin,
How do you do,
  And how do you do,
  And how do you do again!

Rain on the green grass,
  And rain on the tree;
And rain upon the house-top,
  But not upon me!

Rain, rain, go away,
  Come again another day;
Little Johnny wants to play.

Here we go round the mulberry bush,
   The mulberry bush, the mulberry bush,
Here we go round the mulberry bush,
   So early in the morning.

This is the way we clap our hands,
Clap our hands, clap our hands,
This is the way we clap our hands,
   So early in the morning.

This is the way we shake our heads,
Shake our heads, shake our heads,
This is the way we shake our heads,
   So early in the morning.

This is the way we touch our toes,
Touch our toes, touch our toes,
This is the way we touch our toes,
So early in the morning.

This is the way we skip about,
Skip about, skip about,
This is the way we skip about,
So early in the morning.

Three little kittens, they lost their mittens,
    And they began to cry,
"Oh, mother dear, we sadly fear
    That we have lost our mittens."

"What! Lost your mittens, you naughty kittens!
    Then you shall have no pie.
    Mee-ow, mee-ow, mee-ow.
    No, you shall have no pie."

The three little kittens, they found their mittens,
    And they began to cry,
"Oh, mother dear, see here, see here,
    For we have found our mittens."

"Put on your mittens, you silly kittens,
    And you shall have some pie.
    Purr-r, purr-r, purr-r,
    You shall have some pie."

The three little kittens put on their mittens,
And soon ate up the pie.
"Oh, mother dear, we greatly fear
That we have soiled our mittens."

"What! Soiled your mittens, you naughty kittens!"
Then they began to sigh,
"Mee-ow, mee-ow, mee-ow."
Then they began to sigh.

The three little kittens, they washed their mittens
And hung them up to dry.
"Oh, mother dear, do you not hear
That we have washed our mittens?"

"What! Washed your mittens, you good little kittens,
But I smell a rat close by."
"Mee-ow, mee-ow, mee-ow,
We smell a rat close by."

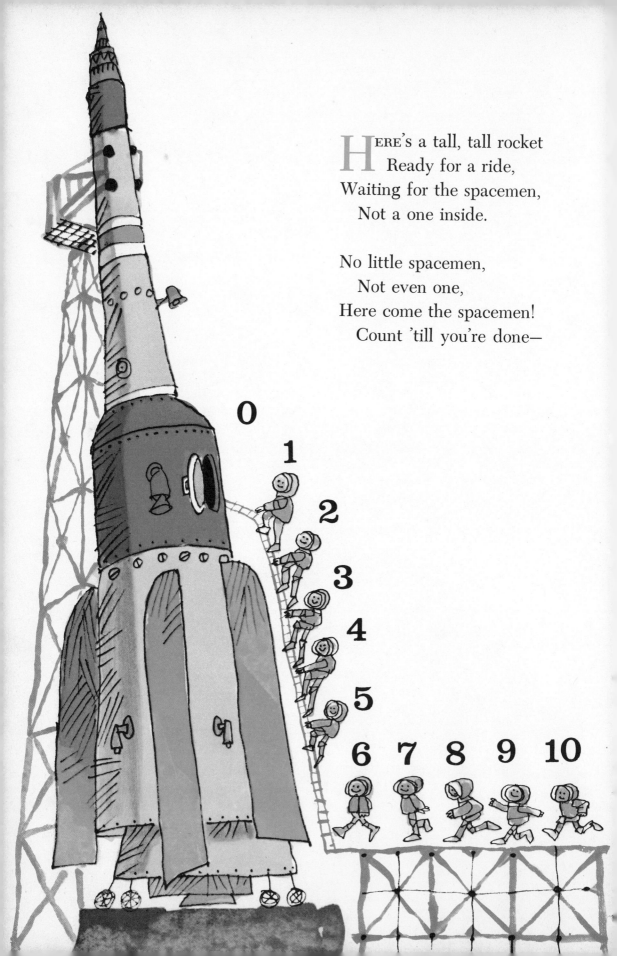

H<small>ERE</small>'s a tall, tall rocket
   Ready for a ride,
Waiting for the spacemen,
   Not a one inside.

No little spacemen,
   Not even one,
Here come the spacemen!
   Count 'till you're done—

0
1
2
3
4
5
6 7 8 9 10

Ten little spacemen
   Ready to zoom,
Here comes the countdown—

10
9
8
7
6
5
4
3
2
1
0

BOOOOM

S TAR light, star bright,
   First star I see tonight,
I wish I may, I wish I might,
Have the wish I wish tonight.

I SEE the moon,
   And the moon sees me;
God bless the moon,
   And God bless me.

Singing-Time

I wake in the morning early
  And always, the very first thing,
I poke out my head and I sit up in bed.
  And I sing and I sing and I sing.

—ROSE FYLEMAN

35

Time to Rise

A birdie with a yellow bill
Hopped upon the window sill,
Cocked his shining eye and said:
"Ain't you 'shamed, you sleepy-head?"

—ROBERT LOUIS STEVENSON

Mix a Pancake

Mix a pancake,
Stir a pancake,
Pop it in the pan;

Fry the pancake,
Toss the pancake,
Catch it if you can.

—CHRISTINA ROSSETTI

Bread and Milk for Breakfast

Bread and milk for breakfast,
  And woolen frocks to wear,
And a crumb for robin redbreast
  On the cold days of the year.

—CHRISTINA ROSSETTI

Morning

Will there really be a morning?
   Is there such a thing as day?
Could I see it from the mountains
   If I were as tall as they?

Has it feet like water-lilies?
   Has it feathers like a bird?
Is it brought from famous countries
   Of which I have never heard?

Oh, some scholar! Oh, some sailor!
   Oh, some wise man from the skies!
Please to tell a little pilgrim
   Where the place called morning lies.

—EMILY DICKINSON

Park Play

Every morning
   I can play
In the park
   Across the way.

I can run
   And I can shout.
I am glad
   When I come out.

—JAMES S. TIPPETT

A Kite

I often sit and wish that I
Could be a kite up in the sky,
And ride upon the breeze and go
Whichever way I chanced to blow.

38

—AUTHOR UNKNOWN

Somersault

I somersault just like a clown
And all the trees turn upside down.

The sky is not the sky at all—
It changes to a high blue wall

And every little buttercup
Looks down at me instead of up.

—DOROTHY ALDIS

I Sail My Boat

I sail my boat on a tiny sea,
   Blow, wind, blow;
And some day I shall a sailor be,
   Blow, wind, blow.

—AUTHOR UNKNOWN

The Ice-Cream Man

When summer's in the city,
  And brick's a blaze of heat,
The Ice-Cream Man with his little cart
  Goes trundling down the street.

Beneath his round umbrella,
  Oh, what a joyful sight,
To see him fill the cones with mounds
  Of cooling brown or white:

Vanilla, chocolate, strawberry,
  Or chilly things to drink
From bottles full of frosty-fizz,
  Green, orange, white, or pink.

His cart might be a flower bed
  Of roses and sweet peas,
The way the children cluster around
  As thick as honeybees.

—RACHEL FIELD

The Postman

The whistling postman swings along.
  His bag is deep and wide,
And messages from all the world
  Are bundled up inside.

The postman's walking up our street.
  Soon now he'll ring my bell.
Perhaps there'll be a letter stamped
  In Asia. Who can tell?

—AUTHOR UNKNOWN

The Sprinkler

The sprinkler is what's fun to see
Underneath our big elm tree.

It whirls around its big wet drops,
First on my mother's pretty phlox
And last on father's hollyhocks.

And all their little faces get
So very, very nice and wet.

And when no one is there to see
I run and get some drops on me.

—DOROTHY ALDIS

Twenty Froggies

Twenty froggies went to school
Down beside a rushy pool.
Twenty little coats of green,
Twenty vests all white and clean.

"We must be in time," said they;
"First we study, then we play;
That is how we keep the rule,
When we froggies go to school."

Master Bullfrog, brave and stern,
Called his classes in their turn,
Taught them how to nobly strive,
Also how to leap and dive.

Polished in a high degree,
As each froggie ought to be,
Now they sit on other logs,
Teaching other little frogs.

—GEORGE COOPER

Hiding

I'm hiding, I'm hiding,
  And no one knows where;
For all they can see is my
  Toes and my hair.

And I just heard my father
  Say to my mother—
"But, darling, he must be
  Somewhere or other.

"Have you looked in the inkwell?"
    And Mother said, "Where?"
"In the *inkwell*," said Father. But
    I was not there.

Then "Wait!" cried my mother—
    "I think that I see
Him under the carpet." But
    It was not me.

"Inside the mirror's
    A pretty good place,"
Said Father and looked, but saw
    Only his face.

"We've hunted," sighed Mother,
    "As hard as we could
And I *am* so afraid that we've
    Lost him for good."

Then I laughed out aloud
    And I wiggled my toes
And Father said—"Look, dear,
    I wonder if those

"Toes could be Benny's.
    There are ten of them. See?"
And they *were* so surprised to find
    Out it was me!

—DOROTHY ALDIS

A Fairy Went A-Marketing

A fairy went a-marketing—
　　She bought a little fish;
She put it in a crystal bowl
　　Upon a golden dish.
An hour she sat in wonderment
　　And watched its silver gleam,
And then she gently took it up
　　And slipped it in a stream.

A fairy went a-marketing—
　　She bought a colored bird;
It sang the sweetest, shrillest song
　　That ever she had heard.
She sat beside its painted cage
　　And listened half the day,
And then she opened wide the door
　　And let it fly away.

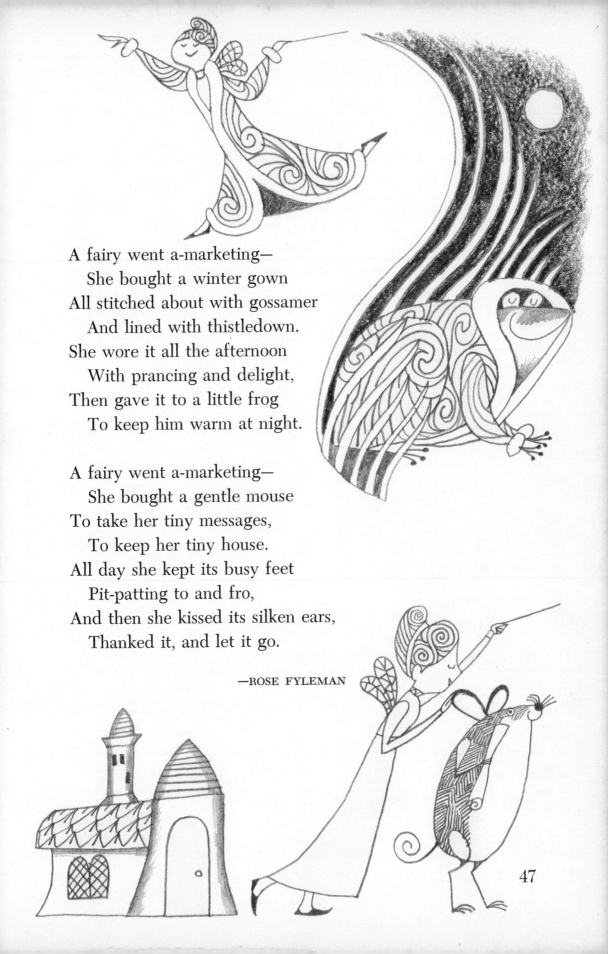

A fairy went a-marketing—
　　She bought a winter gown
All stitched about with gossamer
　　And lined with thistledown.
She wore it all the afternoon
　　With prancing and delight,
Then gave it to a little frog
　　To keep him warm at night.

A fairy went a-marketing—
　　She bought a gentle mouse
To take her tiny messages,
　　To keep her tiny house.
All day she kept its busy feet
　　Pit-patting to and fro,
And then she kissed its silken ears,
　　Thanked it, and let it go.

—ROSE FYLEMAN

Holding Hands

Elephants walking
Along the trails

Are holding hands
By holding tails.

Trunks and tails
Are handy things

When elephants walk
In Circus rings.

Elephants work
And elephants play

And elephants walk
And feel so gay.

And when they walk—
It never fails

They're holding hands
By holding tails.

—LENORE M. LINK

Walking

When Daddy
Walks
With Jean and me,
We have a
Lot of fun
'Cause we can't
Walk as fast
As he,
Unless we
Skip and
Run!
I stretch,
And stretch
My legs so far,
I nearly slip
And fall—
But how
Does Daddy
Take such steps?
He doesn't stretch
At all!

—GRACE GLAUBITZ

Clouds

White sheep, white sheep,
    On a blue hill,
When the wind stops
    You all stand still.
When the wind blows
    You walk away slow.
White sheep, white sheep,
    Where do you go?

—CHRISTINA ROSSETTI

Lilies

I thought I saw white clouds, but no!—
    Bending across the fence,
    White lilies in a row!

—SHIKO 1665-1731

In the Meadow

In the meadow—what is in the meadow?
Bluebells, buttercups, meadowsweet,
And fairy rings for children's feet,
    In the meadow.

—CHRISTINA ROSSETTI

Where Go the Boats?

Dark brown is the river,
Golden is the sand.
It flows along forever,
With trees on either hand.

Green leaves a-floating,
Castles of the foam,
Boats of mine a-boating—
Where will all come home?

On goes the river
And out past the mill,
Away down the valley,
Away down the hill.

Away down the river,
A hundred miles or more,
Other little children
Shall bring my boats ashore.

—ROBERT LOUIS STEVENSON

I Can Be a Tiger

I can't go walking
    When they say no,
And I can't go riding
    Unless they go.
I can't splash puddles
    In my shiny new shoes,
But I can be a tiger
    Whenever I choose.

I can't eat peanuts
    And I can't eat cake,
I have to go to bed
    When they stay awake.
I can't bang windows
    And I mustn't tease,
But I can be an elephant
    As often as I please.

—MILDRED LEIGH ANDERSON

How Creatures Move

The lion walks on padded paws,
  The squirrel leaps from limb to limb,
While flies can crawl straight up a wall,
  And seals can dive and swim.
The worm, he wiggles all around,
  The monkey swings by his tail,
And birds may hop upon the ground,
  Or spread their wings and sail.
But boys and girls have much more fun:
  They leap
    and dance
      and walk
        and run!

—AUTHOR UNKNOWN

53

Little Talk

Don't you think it's probable
  that beetles, bugs, and bees
talk about a lot of things—
  you know, such things as these:

The kind of weather where they live
  in jungles tall with grass
and earthquakes in their villages
  whenever people pass!

Of course, we'll never know if bugs
  talk very much at all,
because our ears are far too big
  for talk that is so small.

—AILEEN FISHER

The Little Turtle

There was a little turtle.
   He lived in a box.
He swam in a puddle.
   He climbed on the rocks.

He snapped at a mosquito.
   He snapped at a flea.
He snapped at a minnow.
   And he snapped at me.

He caught the mosquito.
   He caught the flea.
He caught the minnow.
   But he didn't catch me.

—VACHEL LINDSAY

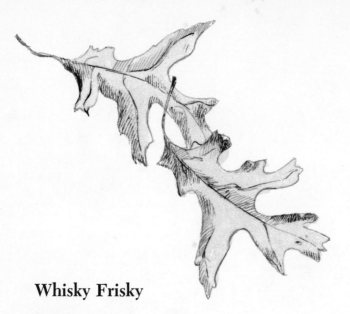

Whisky Frisky

Whisky Frisky,
  Hippity-hop
Up he goes
  To the treetop!

Whirly, twirly
  Round and round,
Down he scampers
  To the ground.

Furly, curly,
  What a tail!
Tall as a feather,
  Broad as a sail!

Where's his supper?
  In the shell,
Snap, cracky,
  Out it fell.

—AUTHOR UNKNOWN

56

The Star

Twinkle, twinkle, little star,
How I wonder what you are,
Up above the world so high,
Like a diamond in the sky!

When the blazing sun is set,
And the grass with dew is wet,
Then you show your little light,
Twinkle, twinkle, all the night.

—JANE TAYLOR

Bed in Summer

In winter I get up at night
And dress by yellow candle-light.
In summer, quite the other way,
I have to go to bed by day.

I have to go to bed and see
The birds still hopping on the tree,
Or hear the grown-up people's feet
Still going past me on the street.

And does it not seem hard to you,
When all the sky is clear and blue,
And I should like so much to play,
To have to go to bed by day?

—ROBERT LOUIS STEVENSON

57

Farewell to the Farm

The coach is at the door at last;
The eager children, mounting fast
And kissing hands, in chorus sing:
"Good-bye, good-bye, to everything!

"To house and garden, field and lawn,
The meadow-gates we swang upon,
To pump and stable, tree and swing,
Good-bye, good-bye, to everything!

"And fare you well for evermore,
O ladder at the hayloft door,
O hayloft where the cobwebs cling,
Good-bye, good-bye, to everything!"

Crack goes the whip, and off we go;
The trees and houses smaller grow;
Last, round the woody turn we swing:
"Good-bye, good-bye, to everything!"

—ROBERT LOUIS STEVENSON

Come, Little Leaves

"Come, little leaves," said the wind one day,
"Come o'er the meadows with me and play;
Put on your dresses of red and gold,
For summer is gone and the days grow cold."

Soon as the leaves heard the wind's loud call,
Down they came fluttering, one and all;
Over the brown fields they danced and flew,
Singing the glad little songs they knew.

"Cricket, good-by. We've been friends so long;
Little brook, sing us your farewell song;
Say you are sorry to see us go;
Ah, you will miss us, right well we know."

Dancing and whirling, the little leaves went;
Winter had called them, and they were content;
Soon, fast asleep in their earthy beds,
The snow laid a coverlid over their heads.

—GEORGE COOPER

Rain

The rain is raining all around,
   It falls on field and tree;
It rains on the umbrellas here,
   And on the ships at sea.

—ROBERT LOUIS STEVENSON

The Umbrella Brigade

"Pitter patter!" falls the rain
On the schoolroom windowpane.
Such a plashing! such a dashing!
Will it e'er be dry again?
Down the gutter rolls a flood,
And the crossing's deep in mud;
And the puddles! oh, the puddles
Are a sight to stir one's blood!

CHORUS.   But let it rain
        Tree-toads and frogs,
        Muskets and pitchforks,
        Kittens and dogs!
        Dash away! plash away!
        Who is afraid?
        Here we go,
        The Umbrella Brigade!

Pull the boots up to the knee!
Tie the hoods on merrily!
Such a hustling! such a jostling!
Out of breath with fun are we.
Clatter, clatter, down the street,
Greeting every one we meet,
With our laughing and our chaffing,
Which the laughing drops repeat.

CHORUS.   So let it rain
           Tree-toads and frogs,
           Muskets and pitchforks,
           Kittens and dogs!
           Dash away! plash away!
           Who is afraid?
           Here we go,
           The Umbrella Brigade!

—LAURA E. RICHARDS

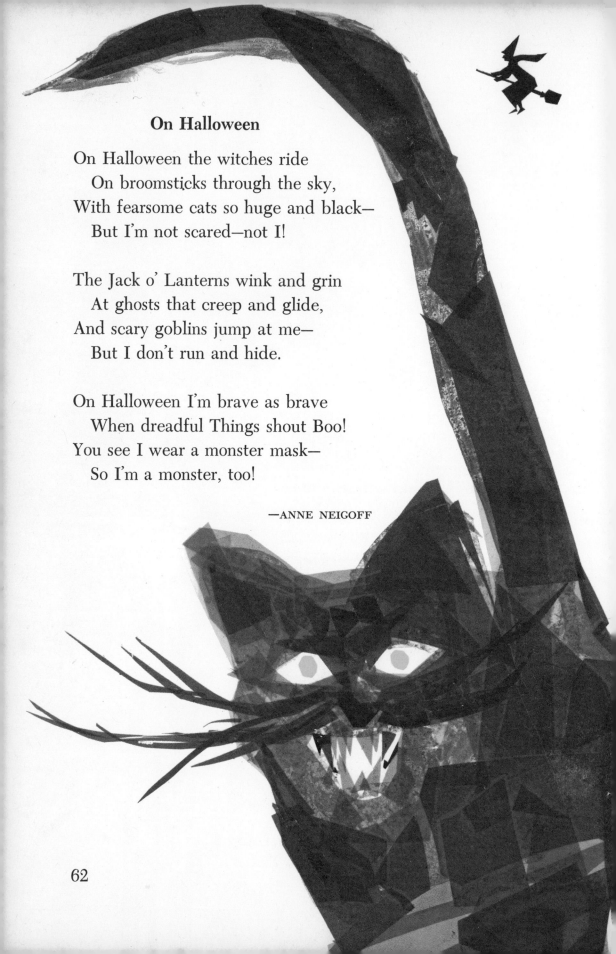

On Halloween

On Halloween the witches ride
  On broomsticks through the sky,
With fearsome cats so huge and black—
  But I'm not scared—not I!

The Jack o' Lanterns wink and grin
  At ghosts that creep and glide,
And scary goblins jump at me—
  But I don't run and hide.

On Halloween I'm brave as brave
  When dreadful Things shout Boo!
You see I wear a monster mask—
  So I'm a monster, too!

—ANNE NEIGOFF

62

The Playhouse Key

This is the key to the playhouse
   In the woods by the pebbly shore,
It's winter now; I wonder if
   There's snow about the door?

I wonder if the fir trees tap
   Green fingers on the pane;
If sea gulls cry and the roof is wet
   And tinkley with rain?

I wonder if the flower-sprigged cups
   And plates sit on their shelf,
And if my little painted chair
   Is rocking by itself?

—RACHEL FIELD

First Thanksgiving of All

Peace and Mercy and Jonathan,
　And Patience (very small),
Stood by the table giving thanks
　The first Thanksgiving of all.
There was very little for them to eat,
Nothing special and nothing sweet;
Only bread and a little broth,
And a bit of fruit (and no tablecloth);
But Peace and Mercy and Jonathan
　And Patience, in a row,
Stood up and asked a blessing on
　Thanksgiving, long ago.

Thankful they were their ship had come
　Safely across the sea;
Thankful they were for hearth and home,
　And kin and company;
They were glad of broth to go with their bread,
Glad their apples were round and red,
Glad of mayflowers they would bring
Out of the woods again next spring.
So Peace and Mercy and Jonathan,
　And Patience (very small),
Stood up gratefully giving thanks
　The first Thanksgiving of all.

—NANCY BYRD TURNER

Long, Long Ago

Winds through the olive trees
　　Softly did blow,
Round little Bethlehem
　　Long, long ago.

Sheep on the hillside lay
　　Whiter than snow;
Shepherds were watching them,
　　Long, long ago.

Then from the happy sky,
　　Angels bent low,
Singing their songs of joy,
　　Long, long ago.

For in a manger bed,
　　Cradled we know,
Christ came to Bethlehem,
　　Long, long ago.

—AUTHOR UNKNOWN

Old Christmas Carol

God bless the master of this house,
    Likewise the mistress too,
And all the little children,
    That round the table go,
And all your kin and kinsmen
    That dwell both far and near;
I wish you a Merry Christmas,
    And a Happy New Year.

—AUTHOR UNKNOWN

Story
Time

The Color Kittens

by Margaret Wise Brown

illustrated by George Suyeoka

Once there were two color kittens with green eyes, Brush and Hush. They liked to mix and make colors by splashing one color into another. They had buckets and buckets and buckets and buckets of color to splash around with. Out of these colors they would make all the colors in the world.

The buckets had the colors written on them, but of course the kittens couldn't read. They had to tell by the colors.

"It is very easy," said Brush.

"Red is red. Blue is blue," said Hush.

But they had no green.

"No green paint!" said Brush and Hush. And they wanted green paint, of course, because nearly every place they liked to go was green.

    Green as cats' eyes
    Green as grass
    By streams of water
    Green as glass.
So they tried to make some green paint.

Brush mixed red paint and white paint together—and what did that make? It didn't make green.

But it made pink.

Pink as pigs
Pink as toes
Pink as a rose
Or a baby's nose.

Then Hush mixed yellow and red together, and it made orange.

> Orange as an orange tree
> Orange as a bumblebee
> Orange as the setting sun
> Sinking slowly in the sea.

The kittens were delighted, but it didn't make green.

Then they mixed red and blue together—and what did that make? It didn't make green. It made a deep dark purple.

> Purple as violets
> Purple as prunes
> Purple as shadows
> On late afternoons.
> Still no green! And then . . .

O wonderful kittens! O Brush! O Hush!

At last, almost by accident, the kittens poured a bucket of blue and a bucket of yellow together, and it came to pass that they made a green as green as grass.

Green as green leaves on a tree
Green as islands in the sea.

The little kittens were so happy with all the colors they had made that they began to paint everything around them.

They painted . . .

Green leaves and red berries
and purple flowers and pink cherries
Red tables and yellow chairs
Black trees with golden pears.

Then the kittens got so excited they knocked their buckets upside down and all the colors ran together. Yellow, red, a little blue and little black . . . and that made brown.

Brown as a tug boat
Brown as an old goat
Brown as a beaver
Brown

And in all that brown, the sun went down. It was evening and the colors began to disappear in the warm dark night.

The kittens fell asleep in the warm dark night with all their colors out of sight and as they slept they dreamed their dream—

A wonderful dream
Of a red rose tree
That turned all white
When you counted three.
One . . . two . . . three
Of a purple land
In a pale pink sea
Where apples fell
From a golden tree
And then a world of Easter eggs
That danced about on little short legs.
And they dreamed
Of a mouse
A little gray mouse
That danced on a cheese
That was big as a house
And a green cat danced
With a little pink dog
Till they all disappeared in a soft gray fog.

And suddenly Brush woke up and Hush woke up. It was morning. They crawled out of bed into a big bright world. The sky was wild with sunshine.

The kittens were wild with purring and pouncing—

pounce

pounce

pounce

They got so pouncy they knocked over the buckets and all the colors ran out together.

There were all the colors in the world and the color kittens had made them.

Sing Ho for the color of Brush

Sing Ho for the color of Hush

Sing Ho for the color of Brush and Hush

Sing Ho for the color of color

Now Hush!

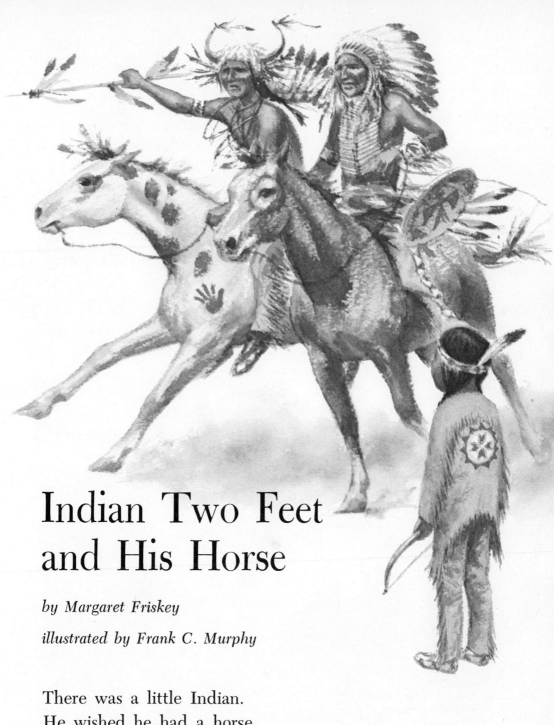

Indian Two Feet
and His Horse

by Margaret Friskey

illustrated by Frank C. Murphy

There was a little Indian.
He wished he had a horse.
But he did not have a horse.
He had to *walk,*
        walk,
           walk.

He could sing.
He could dance.
He could skin a deer for hide.
But he could not ride a horse.
He had to walk.

He could listen to a story.
He could paint with a piece of bone.
But, of course, he had no horse.

He walked to the woods.
He walked to the river.
He walked to the top
of a high, high hill.
And still, he had no horse.

He could ride some rolling rocks.
He could ride a big, fat log.
He could swing across a river from a tree.

But, of course, he could not ride a horse.
He did not have one.

79

"Little Two Feet," said his father. "You must think like a horse to find one. Go find one."

Little Two Feet walked to some tall grass.

"If I were a horse," said Two Feet, "I would put my nose into this grass."

But, oh!

He did not find a horse.

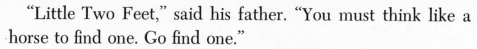

He ran to a river.

"If I were a horse," said Two Feet,
"I would put my nose into this river."

But, oh! No!

He did not find a horse.

He ran to a hill where the sun was hot.

"If I were a horse," said Two Feet, "I would find a cool, cool, spot."

So he sat in the shadow of a big, old rock and went to sleep.

Oh, no! He didn't find a horse. But a horse found him.

Now a horse has four feet but this one stood on three.

He held up a sore foot for Two Feet to see.

"Oh," said Two Feet. "It must be a dream. But if I were a horse, with one bad foot, I would need some help from a boy like me."

Two Feet put his shirt around his horse's leg, to help him hold his sore foot off the ground.

"I will help you," said Two Feet. "Come with me."

Little Two Feet had a horse, but he walked.

They came to a river.
And they both had a drink.
They came to the grass so long and cool.
They rested for a while.
And then they walked.
And at last they both came home.

"Little Two Feet has a horse!"
said his father.
And they all danced and sang.

Every day, Little Two Feet
brought his horse some water.
He brought him some grass.
He worked with that horse's
foot until the foot was well.

And then he *rode* to the woods.
He *rode* to the river.
He *rode* to the top of a high, high hill.
He had a horse!

Angus and the Ducks

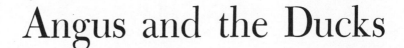

by Marjorie Flack

illustrated by Seymour Fleishman

Once there was a very young little dog whose name was Angus, because his mother and his father came from Scotland.

Although the rest of Angus was quite small, his head was very large and so were his feet.

Angus was curious about many places and many things.

He was curious about *What* lived under the sofa and in dark corners and *Who* was the little dog in the tall mirror.

He was curious about *Things-Which-Come-Apart* and those *Things-Which-Don't-Come-Apart;* such as slippers and gentlemen's suspenders and things like that.

Angus was curious about *Things-Indoors*, and Angus was also curious about *Things-Outdoors* but he could not find out much about them because of a leash.

The leash was fastened at one end to the collar around his neck and at the other end to *Somebody Else*.

But Angus was most curious of all about a *Noise* which came from the other side of the large green hedge at the end of the garden.

The noise usually sounded like this:

Quack! Quack! Quackety! Quack!!

But sometimes it sounded like this:

Quackety! Quackety! Quackety! Quack!!

One day the door between out-doors and indoors was left open by mistake; and out went Angus without the leash or *Somebody Else*.

Down the little path he ran until he came to the large green hedge at the end of the garden.

He tried to go around it but it was much too long. He tried to go over it but it was much too high. So Angus went under the large green hedge and came out on the other side.

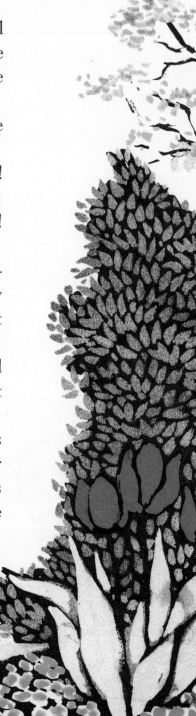

There, directly in front of him, were two white ducks. They were marching forward, one-foot-up and one-foot-down. Quack! Quack! Quackety! Quack!!!

Angus said: WOO-OO-OOF!!!

Away went the two ducks all of a flutter.

Quackety! Quackety! Quackety! Quackety! Quackety!!!

Angus followed after.

Soon the ducks stopped by a stone watering trough under a mulberry tree.

Angus stopped, too. Each duck dipped a yellow bill in the clear cool water. Angus watched. Each duck took a long drink of the cool clear water. Still Angus watched. Each duck took another long drink of cool clear water.

Angus said: WOO-OO-OOF!!!

Away the ducks scuttled and Angus lapped the clear cool water. Birds sang in the mulberry tree. The sun made patterns through the leaves over the grass.

The ducks talked together: Quack! Quack! Quack! Then:

HISS-S-S-S-S-S-S!!!

HISS-S-S-S-S-S-S!!!

The first duck nipped Angus's tail! HISS-S-S-S-S-S-S!!! HISS-S-S-S-S-S-S!!! The second duck flapped her wings!

Angus scrambled under the large green hedge, scurried up the little path, scampered into the house and crawled under the sofa.

For exactly THREE minutes by the clock, Angus was *not* curious about anything at all.

The Three
Billy Goats Gruff

by Asbjörnsen and Moe

illustrated by Ralph Creasman

Once upon a time there were three Billy Goats. One was a
little Billy Goat, one was a middle-sized Billy Goat, and one
was a big Billy Goat; and the name of all three was "Gruff."

One sunny day the three Billy Goats Gruff began to climb
a hill to eat the green grass that grew on the hillside, for they
wanted to make themselves fat.

On the way up the hill was a stream with a bridge over it
that the Billy Goats had to cross. Under the bridge lived a
huge, ugly, fierce Troll. His eyes were big as saucers, and his
nose was as long as a poker.

The little Billy Goat came to the bridge first and started to cross it.

"TRIP, TRAP! TRIP, TRAP!" went the bridge.

"*Who's that* tripping over my bridge?" roared the Troll.

"Oh, it is only I, the teeny, tiny Billy Goat Gruff, and I'm going up to the hillside to eat the green grass that grows there and make myself fat," said the Billy Goat in a very small voice.

"Now I'm coming to gobble you up!" said the Troll.

"Oh, no, don't do that. I'm too little, that I am," said the Billy Goat. "Wait a bit until the second Billy Goat comes. He's MUCH bigger."

"Well," grumbled the Troll. "Go along then."

And the little Billy Goat Gruff crossed the bridge, TRIP, TRAP, TRIP, TRAP, and went up to the hillside to eat the green grass that grew there.

A little while later, the middle-sized Billy Goat Gruff came to the bridge and started to cross it.

"TRIP, TRAP! TRIP, TRAP! TRIP, TRAP!" went the bridge.

"*Who's that* tripping over my bridge?" roared the Troll.

"Oh, it is only I, the middle-sized Billy Goat Gruff, and I'm going up to the hillside to eat the green grass and make myself fat," said the second Billy Goat, and his voice wasn't small but it wasn't big either.

"Now I'm coming to gobble you up!" said the Troll.

"Oh, no, don't do that. I'm too little, that I am," said the Billy Goat. "Wait a bit until the big Billy Goat comes. He's MUCH bigger."

"Very well!" grumbled the Troll. "Go along then."

And the middle-sized Billy Goat Gruff crossed the bridge, TRIP, TRAP, TRIP, TRAP, TRIP, TRAP, and went up to the hillside to eat the green grass that grew there.

Just then the big Billy Goat Gruff came to the bridge and started to cross it.

"TRIP, TRAP! TRIP, TRAP! TRIP, TRAP! TRIP, TRAP!" went the bridge, for the big Billy Goat was so heavy that the bridge creaked and groaned under him.

"*Who's that* tramping over my bridge?" roared the Troll.

"It is I! The Big Billy Goat Gruff!" said the Billy Goat who had a fine roar of his own.

"Now I'm coming to gobble you up!" said the Troll.

"Well, come along!" roared the big Billy Goat Gruff,
"I've got two horns so sharp and bright,
I'll butt you into tomorrow night!
I'll stamp you,
I'll tramp you,
Come along and fight!"

That was what the big Billy Goat said, and he stamped and he tramped across the bridge like thunder. He rushed at the Troll with his sharp, bright horns.

And he butted him once, he butted him twice, he butted him three times and tossed the Troll high in the sky. Did the Troll come down again? He didn't come down that day and he didn't come down that night and if he came down tomorrow night, nobody knows for he was never seen again.

What did the big Billy Goat do then?

After that the big Billy Goat Gruff went up to the hillside. And the three Billy Goats Gruff ate the green grass that grew there. They ate and they ate and they ate and they got so fat, they were scarce able to walk home again. And if the fat hasn't fallen off them, why they're still fat; and so—

"Snip, snap, snout,
This tale's told out."

Here Comes Daddy

by Winifred Milius

illustrated by John Faulkner

A boy named Peter had a cat named Finnigan.

One day just before supper Peter and Finnigan went out to the corner to watch for Peter's Daddy to come home. They looked up and down the street. They saw a lady with a baby carriage, a man sweeping leaves, two boys on a bicycle, and a little spotted dog.

But . . . *no Daddy yet.*

Pretty soon along came someone pushing a little wagon in front of him. Could this be Daddy coming home?

No. It was a delivery boy. He stopped and took some groceries into a yellow house and went away.

No Daddy yet.

A little truck came up the street. Could this be Daddy coming home?

No. It was a bread truck. It stopped in front of the grocery store and the man delivered some bread.

No Daddy yet.

Around the corner came a car. A lady and a dog were in it. Could this be Daddy coming home?

No. The car went by without stopping.

"P-s-s-s-s-s-st!" said Finnigan to the dog.

No Daddy yet.

A big coal truck lumbered up the street. Could this be Daddy coming home?

No. The coal truck stopped at a house. Clankety clank! Coal rattled into barrels. Roll them away, into the cellar.

No Daddy yet.

A great big moving van drove up and stopped. Could this be Daddy coming home?

No. Men got out and carried tables and chairs and lamps and a big couch into a house.

No Daddy yet.

Up the street came a truck squirting water from its sides. Could this be Daddy coming home?

No. It was a street sprinkling truck and water swish-sh-sh-sh-shed all over the street.

No Daddy yet.

Then around the corner came a bus full of people. Could this be Daddy coming home?

The bus stopped and out got a tall, thin lady, a little old man with an umbrella, a boy with a suitcase, and a man carrying a newspaper.

"Here's Daddy, now!" Peter shouted.

Daddy took Peter's hand and Daddy and Peter and Finnigan all walked home together.

Koala Bear Twins

by Inez Hogan

illustrated by Franz Altschuler

High in a gum tree in the Bushland of Australia, there lived
a mother koala bear and she had a secret. None of the other
koala bears in the tree knew about the secret hidden in her
pocket until one day two little heads peeped out! They looked
like Teddy Bears except they were alive.

All the bears in the tree gathered around. How surprised
they were!

"Twins!" said Father Koala proudly.

Mother Koala was proud, too. She took one baby out of
her pocket and held him in her arms.

"This is Kip," she said. "He's a boy." Then she took the other baby in her arms. "This is Tinka. She's a girl."

Then Mother Koala put the twins back in her pouch. They snuggled together, safe and warm—though it was a little crowded with two in one pouch.

Tinka was glad to stay there, but Kip wanted to find out more about the world outside. He climbed out of the pouch into his mother's arms.

"Where are the other koalas?" Kip asked.

"They have moved to another tree," said Mother. "This is our own tree house. Just for our family. Climb on my back and hold tight." And she took Kip for a piggy-back ride all over the tree. Then she put him back in her pouch.

"What did you find out?" asked Tinka.

"I found out we live in a tree," said Kip. "I had a piggy-back ride all over our tree house."

"I want to ride piggy-back, too," said Tinka.

"We'll take turns," said Kip. "Now it's your turn."

So Tinka crawled out. The world outside frightened her a little, but she felt safe in her mother's arms. She looked out at the world with her little black, shoe-button eyes.

She saw a bird light on a branch and she heard laughing—
"Ha-ha-ha! Hoo-oo!"

"What's that?" asked Tinka.

"A kookaburra bird," said Mother.

"Why is he laughing at us?"

"The kookaburra bird laughs all the time," said Mother.
"Now climb on my back and I'll take you for a ride."

"I might fall off," said Tinka.

"You know how to cling." Mother Koala stretched out her
arms. "See, you're clinging now. Cling to my back. I need my
arms for climbing."

Tinka clung to her mother's back and she rode all over the
tree.

Back in the pouch, she told Kip about the kookaburra bird.

"I want to see him," said Kip, and he climbed out of the
pouch just in time to see the kookaburra fly away.

"Will I learn to fly like that?" Kip asked.

"No," said Mother, "you have no wings. But you will learn
to cling and crawl and climb and leap from branch to branch."

"And run?" asked Kip.

"Yes," said Mother, "but you must remember koala bears
are acrobats in the tree, but clumsy on the ground. Never
leave the tree. It would be dangerous for you until you learn
many things. Let's start now. You know how to cling to my
back. Now try to cling to this branch by yourself."

"That's easy," said Kip. But he didn't stay long because he
saw a strange big, big animal standing on the ground.

"What's that?" he asked as soon as he was safe in his mother's arms again.

"That's a kangaroo," said Mother. "Kangaroos are fast on the ground. They can take long, high leaps. But they can't climb trees."

"Look!" said Kip. "She has a baby. He's riding in her pouch just as I do in yours."

And he hurried back into the pouch and told Tinka about the kangaroo. "It's your turn now," Kip said. "Hurry out before the kangaroo goes away."

Tinka climbed out just in time to see the kangaroo leaping over the ground. She watched until it was out of sight. Then Mother Koala carried Tinka to the top of the tree.

Mother reached up and pulled down a small branch of tender leaves and tickled Tinka on the nose.

"They smell good," said Tinka.

"Taste them," said Mother.

"They taste good," said Tinka.

106

"Soon you'll stop drinking milk in my pouch," said Mother. "You'll like gum leaves better."

Tinka peeped into the pouch and called, "Kip, come out! I've found out about something wonderful." And when Kip stuck his nose out, she tickled it with a leaf.

Kip smelled the leaf and tasted it. It was good!

"I'm never going back in the pouch," he said. "I'm not a baby any more."

"That's right," said Mother Koala, giving her twins a big hug. "Now you'll learn to feed yourselves, and soon you'll learn to climb by yourselves. But remember, you must never, never climb out of the tree."

Soon the two little bears were climbing all over the tree. At first Mother Koala followed them. She taught them to leap from bough to bough by giving them a little push.

Kip was daring and mischievous. Once he crawled out on a thin branch. His mother couldn't follow because she was too big. But she climbed to a nearby branch and reached out and pulled him into her arms and smacked him.

Kip squalled, but Mother Koala said, "You must climb on strong, safe branches. The thin ones might break and you'd fall to the ground. Remember that."

The koala bear twins grew bigger and bigger. Father Koala was proud of them. But he wasn't with them all the time. Sometimes he would leave the tree. When he came back, the twins were delighted.

Kip showed his father how he could leap from branch to branch. Tinka curled against her father and asked:

"Where do you go when you leave the tree?"

"To another tree," said Father Koala.

"Will we ever go to another tree?" asked Tinka.

"Yes," he said, "when you're older and stronger and have eaten all the leaves on this tree. Then some night we'll move to a new tree. But you must never leave this tree until your mother takes you away. It's dangerous on the ground."

But one day Kip said, "Let's climb to the bottom of the tree and just look at the ground."

The twins were about halfway down when Tinka said, "Look at that big bird sticking his head through the leaves!"

"What are you?" Kip asked. "Are you a bird?"

"Of course," said the bird. "I'm an emu."

"Can you fly?" Kip asked.

"Of course not. Emus can't fly."

"Then you're not a bird," said Kip.

"Of course I am," said the emu. "I'm the second largest bird in the world."

"What a long neck you have," said Tinka.

"I have long legs, too," said the emu.

The twins climbed down until they could see long legs.

"You're a bird all right," said Kip. "You have claws like a bird. Can you run fast with your long legs?"

"Of course," said the emu. "I'll show you." And he ran so fast he was soon out of sight.

Just then Tinka saw something else. "Look!" she said. "I wonder what that is. It's beautiful!"

"That's a lyre bird," said a kookaburra who had just perched on a branch above them. "He can imitate anything. Listen." He laughed. "Ha-ha-hoo-hoo!"

"Ha-ha-hoo-hoo!" laughed the lyre bird.

"Gr-r-r," growled Kip.

"Gr-r-r," growled the lyre bird.

"There are wonderful things in the world," said Tinka.

The two little koala bears climbed further down the tree—almost to the bottom.

"Look," said Tinka. "There's a stream of water beside our tree. A bird is swimming in the water."

The kookaburra laughed. "That's not a bird. It's a platypus, the funniest animal in Australia."

"You laugh at everything," said Kip. "What's so funny about the platypus? He can swim. Can you?"

"Wait until he comes out of the water," said the kookaburra. "You'll see."

The platypus dived down to the bottom of the stream.

"He's eating," said the kookaburra. "He gets his food from the bottom of the stream. Look! Now he's coming up again. He's crawling out of the water."

"Oh," said Tinka. "He's not a bird. He has fur."

"And a long, flat tail," said Kip.

"And webbed feet like a duck," said the kookaburra. "See, he has claws, too. He's digging a hole in the ground. He lives

under the ground. But he has no wings, so he can't fly like me!"

"Tinka," said Kip. "Let's just touch the ground."

"But Mother said we must never leave the tree."

"We won't," said Kip. "We'll just hang from a low branch—like this. And we'll reach down."

Kip held on to the low branch. Tinka crawled out on it, too. Now two little bears are heavier than one little bear so the branch broke—and down they fell, bump, bump!

Tinka began to cry. The kookaburra began to laugh.

"Quiet," whispered Kip. "Mother is asleep up in the tree. She'll wake and hear and see us. We're out of the tree. We're on the ground. And I want to run!"

"Better stay close to the tree," warned the kookaburra. And he flew away.

The little koala bears looked around.

"I don't see anything dangerous," said Kip. "We'll run around the tree just once. Let's go!"

The two little bears ran around the tree—around and around and around.

High up in the tree, Mother Koala woke up suddenly. She heard the Dingo dog howling. Dingos are wild dogs and will eat koalas if they can catch them.

Mother Koala looked for her twins. Then she looked down. She saw her little bears running around the tree. She saw the Dingo coming.

"The Dingo! The Dingo!" she cried. "Climb—climb up the tree!"

Kip and Tinka saw the big dog coming, too. Squalling with fright, they climbed up, up in the tree. They were halfway up when their mother reached them.

The Dingo was howling at the foot of the tree.

"Don't be afraid," said Mother Koala. "You're safe now. Dingo can't climb trees—which is lucky for you. But this is not lucky for you . . ."

She spanked Kip. She spanked Tinka, too.

"We just wanted to find out what was on the ground," squalled Kip and Tinka.

"Well, you found out," said Mother Koala.

Then she hugged her little bears because she was so glad they were safe. And they went to sleep in their mother's arms because they had found out it was the safest place of all.

Chie and the Sports Day

by Masako Matsuno

illustrated by George Suyeoka

"Why should we take her? It's no fun to play with a girl," Michio said to Ichiro.

"I won't play with you if she goes with us," said Hiroshi, and the two boys ran away.

Ichiro looked back at Chie for a moment, then he too ran after the boys.

Chie rubbed the tears from her eyes and watched the boys disappear. Bright dragonflies flew around her head in a friendly way, but Chie was lonely.

Chie kicked a stone, and then another. The stones rolled merrily, chasing each other. But Chie had no one to chase.

It seemed she was always alone these days. Kicking stones, Chie went home.

Before, Ichiro had often played *mamagoto*, or house, with Chie. He had pretended to eat the food Chie made with leaves and flowers. And Ichiro took Chie with him on butterfly hunts.

But everything changed when Ichiro became a schoolboy. He no longer played mamagoto with Chie. Now, every day after school, Ichiro played with his school friends.

Once in a while, not very often, Ichiro took Chie out to play with him, and they raced. But soon, "Crybaby, you're too slow," Ichiro would say, clicking his tongue. And he would run away to join his friends, just as he had today.

Chie opened the kitchen door slowly.

"Chie? Is it you?" Mother called, hearing her footsteps.

But Chie didn't answer. She didn't want to see Mother. She knew just what Mother would say.

"Don't cry, Chie. Ichiro will play with you tomorrow."

Always, she said the same thing, but tomorrow never came. Chie knew it wouldn't.

"Chie?" Mother called louder. "Come in, Chie, and taste this."

Chie opened her eyes wide in surprise.

There on the table were sandwiches, cakes, bananas and apples, chocolate candies, *sushi* rice cakes . . .

"Is it a picnic?" Chie asked.

"No."

"A party?"

"No."

"What? What are these for?"

"Sports day!" Mother said merrily.

"Sports day?"

"Yes. Ichiro's sports day at school tomorrow. Didn't he tell you about it?"

"No, nothing. Can I go?"

"Yes," Mother answered, busily cutting more sandwiches. "You and I are going tomorrow."

"Tomorrow! Oh, tomorrow!" Chie cried, and skipped for joy.

Ichiro, too, was surprised to see the splendid lunch when he came in from play.

"It's for sports day tomorrow," Mother explained.

"But why three lunches?"

"One for me," said Chie excitedly.

"And for me too," Mother added, smiling at Ichiro.

"But you said you couldn't come! You said you had to attend an important meeting!"

"Yes, but I'll cut it short. It's your first sports day. I want to be there," said Mother.

"And me too," Chie cried.

Ichiro looked at Chie.

Then, without a word, he turned and ran to his room.

The whole house shook as Ichiro slammed the door and threw himself on the floor.

Chie was coming to the sports day.

No, he couldn't bear it.

It will be awful, Ichiro thought bitterly.

She will see me running last. Last!

Always, when Ichiro and Chie raced together, Ichiro won.

"Ichiro-*Niichan*, Elder Brother, is so fast," Chie would say admiringly.

But at school Ichiro was almost always the slowest runner of his class.

Chie did not know it.

Ichiro didn't want Chie to know it.

He wanted to keep it secret. He didn't care if anyone else knew he was a slow runner.

But not Chie.

"She shouldn't come," said Ichiro, thumping his feet. "No, she shouldn't. Oh, I hope Mother can't get there in time."

Sports day was a beautiful autumn day. The music of the opening march soared into the deep blue October sky, and under the gay buntings girls danced.

"All first-grade boys! Fall in at the starting gate," called the teacher of athletics over the microphone.

"Please, please . . ." Ichiro prayed to himself as he took his place. "Don't let them be here yet."

His eyes searched the crowd. No, he didn't see them. Goody, they couldn't make it! Ichiro smiled secretly.

The first-grade boys were divided into groups.

"*Yo-o-i! Don!!* Ready! Go!" The first group ran!

"*Yo-o-i! Don!!*" The second group ran!

Now!

"*Yo-o-i! Don!!*" The third group ran! Ichiro ran!

Ichiro forgot all about Mother and Chie. He ran as he had never run before. But soon everyone in his group was ahead of him. He was slow as usual.

"No matter," said Ichiro to himself, running. "No Mother, no Chie, no Mother, no Chie . . ."

The yellow tape for the next group was already up when, his heart beating fast, he ran through the goal.

"Ichiro-*Niichan*!"

"Ichiro!"

Mother and Chie! They had just come in.

"You were the first, *Niichan*, Elder Brother!" Chie called.

"No! Last!" Ichiro shouted.

"Last?" Chie was puzzled.

"Yes! Last!"

And seizing his lunch box Ichiro ran away to join his friends.

During all of lunch time, Ichiro stayed away from Mother and Chie.

The obstacle races began in the afternoon. Anyone who chose could join these games. Barrels, ladders, nets, and other obstacles were placed on the course, and near the end were scattered slips of paper.

After a racer cleared all the other obstacles, the words on his slip told him what to do next. "Get a yellow cap" or "Find a man's shoe" or "Tie this rope."

Look! People burst into laughter. Over there, a fat man was caught in a ladder. He began running with it around his plump stomach.

Ichiro enjoyed obstacle races. It was nothing for him to creep under a net or crawl through a ladder. He picked up his slip of paper.

"Find a little girl and run three-legged with her," it read.

"Chie! Chie, come quickly!"

Ichiro stopped right in front of Chie's seat.

"What is it? What's wrong?" asked Mother in a worried voice.

"I need a little girl to run with me three-legged."

"*Me!* Not me?"

"Yes, you!"

"Oh yes, I'll go with you!" Chie ran to her brother. "Hurry, hurry, Ichiro-*Niichan!*"

Ichiro quickly tied his right foot to Chie's left foot with his head band.

One, two . . . one, two . . . Carefully, the two started.

Now, faster! One, two; one, two; one, two; one, two; one—

Ah! Ichiro stumbled and fell, dragging Chie with him to the ground. Red blood ran on her knees.

"Oh . . . !" Ichiro exclaimed. Now they would be out of the race. Chie would cry and run back to Mother.

"Hurry! Let's go! *Niichan,* please hurry!"

Chie pulled Ichiro's hand.

Together, Chie and Ichiro ran. One, two . . . one, two . . . Left, right; left, right . . . One two; one two . . . They ran and ran. And it was not until he was untying their feet at the end of the course that Ichiro realized they were first.

"Tra-ra-ra . . ."

The music began again, and Ichiro and Chie walked together proudly to receive the first prize.

It was only then, at the retiring gate, that Chie noticed her bloody knees. Tears welled up in her eyes.

"Come," said Ichiro. He carried Chie on his back to the
nurse.

"Does it hurt?"

"No, not much."

Outside, the sun seemed even brighter than before. Ichiro
walked slowly for Chie's sake.

"You won. You won first prize!" said Chie, looking up at
Ichiro.

"I? No, we!" Ichiro replied, smiling. "Half of the prize is
yours. Take these notebooks and pencils. And you can have
the whole box of crayons."

"Really?"

"Yes, really."

Chie was very, very happy.

"Look, Mother," she called. "My notebooks, my pencils.
And a whole box of crayons! I ran with Ichiro-*Niichan*, and
we were first."

126

And Ichiro was happy too.

Why?

Because he won first prize, of course.

But not only because of that.

Can you guess why?

"Tr-ra-ra . . ." the music was still playing. Ichiro skipped to the music to meet his friends.

It was a beautiful autumn day. A deep blue October sky and bright, golden sunshine. Bang! Bang! Up went the fire-crackers. Bang! Bang! Bang!

The games went on.

Mr. Apple
Names the
Children

by Jean McDevitt

illustrated by Dan Siculan

Mr. and Mrs. Apple lived in the city. They lived in a little apartment in a big apartment house. They had lived there a long time. When Mr. and Mrs. Apple first went to live in the city there were not any little Apples. Now there were five little Apples.

The oldest Apple boy was named MacIntosh. This was Mr. Apple's idea. He said there was no use having a name like Apple if you just called your children by ordinary names.

"George Apple or Tom Apple or Jack Apple would not do at all," said Mr. Apple. So the Apple children were named for real apples.

Mrs. Apple did not like this idea of Mr. Apple's very much.

"MacIntosh is much too big a name for a tiny baby," said Mrs. Apple.

"He will not be a tiny baby long," said Mr. Apple. "We will call him Mac for short."

Mrs. Apple saw that Mr. Apple wanted very much to call the baby MacIntosh. "Very well," said Mrs. Apple. "We will call him Mac." She knew she could not have her own way all the time. Mr. Apple must sometimes have what he wanted. So when the second little Apple came he was named Jonathan. He was called Jon for short.

Mrs. Apple got used to the idea of MacIntosh and Jonathan for her two boys. She even boasted a little bit to her neighbors.

"Mr. Apple is very clever," Mrs. Apple would say. "He has such fine ideas. No one but a man as clever as Mr. Apple would have thought of naming his children for real apples."

Then the first little girl came along. It was much harder for Mr. Apple to think of an apple name for a little girl.

"If she had been a boy," said Mr. Apple, "I could have named her Spitzenberg. She could have been Spitz for short."

"She is not a boy and she cannot be named Spitzenberg," said Mrs. Apple. "A little girl should have a pretty name. She cannot be called Spitz."

"How would Delicious be?" asked Mr. Apple. "There is a fine apple named Delicious."

"Delicious is a beautiful name," said Mrs. Apple happily "I think we will call her Delia for short."

The fourth little Apple was also a girl. Mr. Apple had a very hard time indeed to find an apple name for her. He thought and thought about it. But he could not think of an apple name for another little girl.

One day Mr. Apple said to Mrs. Apple, "I know what I will do. I will go to the library and look for a name in a book."

"In a book!" said Mrs. Apple. "Is there a book with apple names in it?"

"Yes," said Mr. Apple. "I am sure there is. There is a book for everything in the library."

So Mr. Apple went to the public library. He said to the Librarian, "Have you a book that will tell me the names of apples?"

"Yes, indeed," said the Librarian. "We have a Garden Encyclopedia."

Mr. Apple took the big book and sat down at a table. He hunted and hunted through it for an apple name for his second little girl. He wrote many names on a piece of paper. Then he took the Garden Encyclopedia back to the Librarian.

"Thank you for your help," said Mr. Apple.

"Did you find what you wanted?" asked the Librarian.

"Well," said Mr. Apple, "I found a great many names, but they are not very good names for a little girl."

The Librarian looked very surprised. "I thought you wanted names of apples," she said.

"So I did, so I did," answered Mr. Apple.

He did not stop to explain. He wanted to get home. He wanted to see if Mrs. Apple would like any of the names he had found.

"Did you find a book of apple names?" asked Mrs. Apple, as soon as Mr. Apple came home.

"Oh yes," said Mr. Apple. "There is a big, big book of apple names in the library. It is called a Garden Encyclopedia."

"It was very clever of you to think of going to the library, Mr. Apple," said Mrs. Apple.

"That is what a library is for," said Mr. Apple.

"What names did you find?" asked Mrs. Apple anxiously.

"Well," said Mr. Apple, "that is the trouble. There were many fine apple names for little boys. If she were a boy, we could call her Fall Pippin or Baldwin. I am very fond of Baldwin apples," said Mr. Apple. "If she were only a boy I would name her Baldwin. We could call her Baldy for short."

"She is not a boy," said Mrs. Apple. "And she cannot be called Baldwin. She cannot be called Baldy. She is a sweet little girl. I am glad she is a little girl. I like little girls."

"I like little girls, too," said Mr. Apple. "But it is so hard to find good names for them."

Mrs. Apple did not say that of course the baby could be called Nancy or Mary or Elizabeth. She did not want to hurt Mr. Apple's feelings.

"What were some of the other names in the Garden Encyclopedia?" asked Mrs. Apple.

"There is an apple called a Snow Apple," said Mr. Apple.

"Snow Apple," said Mrs. Apple. "Snow Apple," she said again. "That is very pretty. I think we will name the baby Snow. She will not need a nickname."

Mr. Apple was very pleased that Mrs. Apple liked one of the names he had found. Snow was a good name for the baby. She had very white skin and bright red cheeks. She looked very much like a little round snow apple. Mr. and Mrs. Apple were very happy to have found just the right name for the fourth little Apple.

After a while the fifth little Apple came. The fifth little Apple was a girl, too! Poor Mr. Apple was quite upset again.

"Oh, dear, oh, dear," he said. "I cannot possibly think of another apple name for a little girl."

"Why not go to the library again?" asked Mrs. Apple.

"No, it would not do any good," said Mr. Apple. "I wrote down all the apple names there were in the Garden Encyclopedia. There was not another name for a little girl."

134

"Well," said Mrs. Apple, "four of our children have apple names. Why not just name this baby girl Nancy or Mary or Elizabeth?"

"No, no," said Mr. Apple. "Those names will not do for an Apple child. I do wish I could think of an apple name for another little girl."

"There!" said Mrs. Apple in excitement. "An Apple—An Apple."

Mr. Apple looked at Mrs. Apple in great surprise.

"What do you mean by saying an apple over and over again?" he asked.

"Why, don't you see?" replied Mrs. Apple. "We can call the fifth baby An Apple. We will spell it An-n. Ann Apple is her name."

Now Mr. Apple saw that Mrs. Apple wanted very much to call the little girl Ann. He did not like this idea of Mrs. Apple's so very much. But Mr. Apple knew that he could not always have what he wanted. Mrs. Apple must sometimes have what she wanted. So Mr. Apple said,

"Ann Apple is not a bad name. At least it makes sense. Nancy Apple or Mary Apple or Elizabeth Apple would not make sense at all."

So the fifth and last little Apple had a real little girl's name, and that pleased Mrs. Apple very much indeed.

The Pancake

by Asbjörnsen and Moe

illustrated by Vernon McKissack

Once on a time there was a goody who had seven hungry
bairns, and she was frying a pancake for them. It was a
sweet-milk pancake, and there it lay in the pan bubbling
and frizzling so thick and good, it was a sight for sore eyes to
look at. And the bairns stood round about, and the goodman
sat by and looked on.

"Oh, give me a bit of pancake, mother, dear; I am so hungry," said one bairn.

"Oh, darling mother," said the second.

"Oh, darling, good mother," said the third.

"Oh, darling, good, nice mother," said the fourth.

"Oh, darling, good, nice, pretty mother," said the fifth.

"Oh, darling, good, nice, pretty, clever mother," said the
sixth bairn.

"Oh, darling, good, nice, pretty, clever, sweet mother," said
the seventh.

So they begged for the pancake all round, the one more
prettily than the other; for they were so hungry and so good.

"Yes, yes, bairns, only bide a bit till it turns itself,"--she ought to have said, "till I can get it turned,"—"and then you shall all have some—a lovely sweet-milk pancake; only look how fat and happy it lies there."

When the pancake heard that it got afraid, and in a trice it turned itself all of itself, and tried to jump out of the pan; but it fell back into it again t'other side up, and so when it had been fried a little on the other side too, till it got firmer in its flesh, it sprang out on the floor, and rolled off like a wheel through the door and down the hill.

"Helloa! Stop, pancake!" and away went the goody after it, with the frying-pan in one hand and the ladle in the other, as fast as she could, and her bairns before her, while the goodman limped after them all.

"Hi, won't you stop? Seize it. Stop, pancake," they all screamed out, one after the other, and tried to catch it on the run and hold it; but the pancake rolled on and on, and in the twinkling of an eye it was so far ahead that they couldn't see it, for the pancake was faster on its feet than any of them.

So when it had rolled a while it met a man.

"Good day, pancake," said the man.

"God bless you, Manny Panny!" said the pancake.

"Dear pancake," said the man, "don't roll so fast; stop a little and let me eat you."

"When I have given the slip to Goody Poody, and the goodman, and seven squalling children, I may well slip through your fingers, Manny Panny," said the pancake and rolled on and on till it met a hen.

"Good day, pancake," said the hen.

"The same to you, Henny Penny," said the pancake.

"Pancake, dear, don't roll so fast, but bide a bit and let me eat you up," said the hen.

"When I have given the slip to Goody Poody, and the goodman, and seven squalling children, and Manny Panny, I may well slip through your claws, Henny Penny," said the pancake, and so it rolled on like a wheel down the road.

Just then it met a cock.

"Good day, pancake," said the cock.

"The same to you, Cocky Locky," said the pancake.

"Pancake, dear, don't roll so fast, but bide a bit and let me eat you up."

"When I have given the slip to Goody Poody, and the good-man, and seven squalling children, and to Manny Panny, and Henny Penny, I may well slip through your claws, Cocky Locky," said the pancake, and off it set rolling away as fast as it could; and when it had rolled a long way it met a duck.

"Good day, pancake," said the duck.

"The same to you, Ducky Lucky."

"Pancake, dear, don't roll away so fast; bide a bit and let me eat you up."

"When I have given the slip to Goody Poody, and the goodman, and seven squalling children, and Manny Panny,

and Henny Penny, and Cocky Locky, then I may well slip through your fingers, Ducky Lucky," said the pancake, and with that it took to rolling and rolling faster than ever; and when it had rolled a long, long while, it met a goose.

"Good day, pancake," said the goose.

"The same to you, Goosey Poosey."

"Pancake, dear, don't roll so fast; bide a bit and let me eat you up."

"When I have given the slip to Goody Poody, and the goodman, and seven squalling children, and Manny Panny, and Henny Penny, and Cocky Locky, and Ducky Lucky, I can well slip through your feet, Goosey Poosey," said the pancake, and off it rolled. So when it had rolled a long, long way farther it met a gander.

"Good day, pancake," said the gander.

"The same to you, Gander Pander," said the pancake.

"Pancake, dear, don't roll so fast; bide a bit and let me eat you up."

"When I have given the slip to Goody Poody, and the goodman, and seven squalling children, and Manny Panny, and Henny Penny, and Cocky Locky, and Ducky Lucky, and Goosey Poosey, I may well slip through your feet, Gander Pander," said the pancake, which rolled off as fast as ever.

So when it had rolled a long, long time, it met a pig.

"Good day, pancake," said the pig.

"The same to you, Piggy Wiggy," said the pancake, which without a word more, began to roll and roll and roll like mad.

"Nay, nay," said the pig, "you needn't be in such a hurry; we two can then go side by side and see one another over the wood; they say it is not too safe in there."

The pancake thought there might be something in that, and so they kept company. But when they had gone awhile, they came to a brook. As for Piggy, he was so fat he swam safe across, it was nothing to him; but the poor pancake couldn't get over.

"Seat yourself on my snout," said the pig, "and I'll carry you over."

So the pancake did that.

"Ouf, ouf," said the pig, and swallowed the pancake at one gulp; and then, as the poor pancake could go no farther, why—this story can go no farther either.

Six Foolish Fishermen

Based on a folktale in Ashton's Chap-books of the Eighteenth Century, 1882

by Benjamin Elkin

illustrated by Joseph Rogers

Once there were six brothers who decided to go fishing. So they went to the river and picked good spots from which to fish.

"I will sit in this boat," said the first brother.

"And I will kneel on this raft," said the second brother.

"And I will lean on this log," said the third brother.

"And I will stand on this bridge," said the fourth brother.

"And I will lie on this rock," said the fifth brother.

"And I will walk on this bank," said the sixth brother.

And that is exactly what they did.

143

Each brother fished from the spot he had chosen, and each one had good luck.

But when it was time to go home, the brothers became a little worried.

"We have been near the river, and over the river, and on the river," said the brother in the boat. "One of us might easily have fallen into the water and been drowned. I shall count all the brothers to be sure there are six of us."

And he began to count:

"I see one brother on the raft. That's *one*.

And another on the log. That's *two*.

And another on the bridge. That's *three*.

And another on the rock. That's *four*.

And another on the bank. That's *five*.

Only *five!* Woe is me. We have lost a brother!" In his sorrow he didn't even notice that he had forgotten to count himself.

"Can it really be?" cried the brother on the raft. "Has one of us been drowned, and have we really lost a brother?"

And he, too, began to count:
"I see one brother on the log. That's *one*.
And another on the bridge. That's *two*.
And another on the rock. That's *three*.
And another on the bank. That's *four*.
And another in the boat. That's *five*.
Only *five*. What will our dear mother say?"
And he, too, didn't even notice that he had forgotten to count himself.

"Let me check from here!" cried the brother on the log.
"I see one brother on the bridge. That's *one*.
And another on the rock. That's *two*.
And another on the bank. That's *three*.
And another in the boat. That's *four*.
And another on the raft. That's *five*.

Five in *all*, oh, unhappy day! Why did we ever come here,
for one of us to be drowned?"

Then the fourth brother counted, and the fifth and the sixth—each one counted only five brothers because each forgot to include himself.

All the brothers went back to the shore and rushed sadly up and down the river's edge, trying to see the body of their poor drowned brother.

Then along came a boy who had also been fishing, but who had not caught a single fish.

"What's the matter?" he asked. "You seem to have plenty of fish. Why do you all look so sad?"

"Because six of us came here to fish, and now there are only five of us left. One of our dear brothers has been drowned!"

The boy looked puzzled. "What do you mean, only five left? How do you figure that?"

"Look, I'll show you," said the eldest brother, and he pointed to his brothers:

"One.

Two.

Three.

Four.

Five.

"Six of us came here, and now only five are going back. Sad is the day!"

The boy turned to hide his smile, and then he turned back. "I think I can help you find your lost brother," he said. "When I squeeze your hand, I want you to count."

As hard as he could he squeezed the hand of each of the brothers, in turn.

"*One!*" yelled the first brother, and he rubbed his aching hand.

"*Two!*" cried the second brother, and he jumped up and down because of the hard squeeze.

"*Three!*" shouted the third brother.

"*Four!*" shrieked the fourth brother.

"*Five!*" screamed the fifth brother.

"*Six!*" roared the sixth brother.

SIX! The brothers looked at each other in delight.

There were six of them again!

They cheered for joy, and slapped each other on the back.

150

Gratefully, they turned to the boy. "Here," they said. "We insist that you take all of our fish. We can never thank you enough for finding our dear, lost brother."

As the boy happily accepted their gift, the six foolish fishermen went their merry way.

The White Goat

by Margery Clark

illustrated by Donald G. Wheeler

One fine Saturday morning Andrewshek's Auntie Katushka said, "Andrewshek, I must go to market and buy a goat."

Andrewshek was playing in the garden. He had pulled out some of the feathers from his fine feather bed and had put them in his hair. He looked very funny.

As Andrewshek's Auntie Katushka went out of the gate to go to market, Andrewshek said, "May I go with you, Auntie Katushka?"

"No, Andrewshek!" said his Auntie Katushka. "You must stay at home. Please watch to see that the dog does not open the gate and let the chickens and the cat run out into the road."

"Yes, indeed, I will watch to see that the dog does not open the gate. And I will be sure that the chickens and the cat do not run out into the road."

Then Auntie Katushka, in her bright shawl, hurried off to market. But all Andrewshek really did was to swing backward and forward on the dark green gate.

152

Andrewshek loved to swing backward and forward on the gate just as much as he loved to bounce up and down on his fine feather bed.

At the market Auntie Katushka saw a white goat. The white goat had a long beard and a short tail. "That is just the goat I want!" said Auntie Katushka.

"White Goat!" said Auntie Katushka, "I am going to take you home with me to Andrewshek."

"Who is Andrewshek?" said the goat.

"Andrewshek is a little boy who lives across the tracks and up the hill, in a little house with a dark green gate. Andrewshek loves to swing backward and forward and backward and forward on the dark green gate."

"I would not be surprised if Andrewshek was swinging backward and forward on the green gate now," said the goat to herself. "I think I'll run ahead and see."

She galloped off.

"Stop, White Goat!" cried Aunt Katushka. "Stop!"

But the goat did not stop. She ran faster and faster, across the tracks and up the hill until she came to the little house with the dark green gate. Andrewshek was swinging backward and forward and backward and forward on the dark green gate. The chickens and the cat had long before run out into the road.

"How do you do, Andrewshek?" said the white goat.

"How do you do, White Goat?" said Andrewshek. "Where are you going?"

"No further!" said the white goat. "I belong to your Auntie Katushka."

"Where is my Auntie Katushka?" said Andrewshek.

"I ran away from her, across the tracks and up the hill; and here I am!" said the goat.

"Won't Auntie Katushka be surprised when she sees you here!" said Andrewshek.

154

"I think I will hide!" said the white goat. She ran behind the little house.

Andrewshek's Aunt Katushka, in her bright shawl, came hurrying up the hill.

"Andrewshek, I bought a sweet white goat at the market to give us milk for our poppy seed cakes. She ran away and so we cannot have any poppy seed cakes today. I wonder how we can find her!"

"Ha! ha! ha!" the sweet white goat called out. She had climbed to the top of the roof where she could look down on Andrewshek and Auntie Katushka.

"Come down from the roof, you naughty White Goat!" said Auntie Katushka. The goat shook her head.

"Please come down!" said Andrewshek. "And I will give you a big poppy seed cake."

"I do not like poppy seed cakes," said the naughty white goat.

"What shall we do?" said Andrewshek.

Andrewshek's Auntie Katushka went into the house and took off her bright shawl. She put on her apron.

She washed some turnips and some parsnips, two onions and four carrots for the soup. Then she cut the green tops from the vegetables. She put the green tops in a basket. "Goats love fresh green tops," she said to Andrewshek, as she put the basket on the back porch by the door. She left the door wide open.

The naughty white goat was peeping over the roof to see what she could see. She saw the green tops in the basket by the kitchen door. Immediately she felt very hungry. She clambered down from the roof. She stole up to the basket.

"Well! well!" laughed Andrewshek's Auntie Katushka, as she slipped a halter around the white goat's neck. "We soon shall have plenty of milk for our poppy seed cakes."

Gone Is Gone

by Wanda Gág

illustrated by George Armstrong

This is an old, old story which my grandmother told me when I was a little girl. When she was a little girl her grandfather had told it to her, and when he was a little peasant boy in Bohemia, his mother had told it to him. And where she heard it, I don't know, but you can see it is an old, old story, and here it is, the way my grandmother used to tell the story.

It is called *Gone Is Gone* and it is the story of a man who wanted to do housework.

157

This man, his name was Fritzl—his wife, her name was Liesi. They had a little baby, Kinndli by name, and Spitz who was a dog. They had one cow, two goats, three pigs, and of geese they had a dozen. That's what they had. They lived on a patch of land, and that's where they worked.

Fritzl had to plow the ground,
sow the seeds and hoe the weeds.

He had to cut the hay and
rake it too, and stack it up in
bunches in the sun.

The man worked hard, you see,
from day to day.

Liesi had the house to clean,
the soup to cook,
the butter to churn,
the barnyard and the baby
to care for.

She, too, worked hard each day
as you can plainly see.

They both worked hard, but Fritzl always thought that he
worked harder. Evenings when he came home from the field
he sat down, mopped his face with his big red handkerchief,
and said: "Hu! How hot it was in the sun today, and how
hard I did work. Little do you know, Liesi, what a man's work
is like, little do you know! Your work now, 'tis nothing at all."

" 'Tis none too easy," said Liesi.

"None too easy!" cried Fritzl. "All you do is to putter and
potter around the house a bit—surely there's nothing hard
about such things."

159

"Nay, if you think so," said Liesi, "we'll take it turn and turn about tomorrow. I will do your work, you can do mine. I will go out in the fields and cut the hay, you can stay here at home and putter and potter around. You wish to try it—yes?"

Fritzl thought he would like that well enough—to lie on the grass and keep an eye on his Kinndli-girl, to sit in the cool shade and churn, to fry a bit of sausage and cook a little soup. Ho! That would be easy! Yes, yes, he'd try it.

Well, Liesi lost no time the next morning. There she was at peep of day, striding out across the fields with a jug of water in her hand and the scythe over her shoulder.

And Fritzl, where was he? He was in the kitchen, frying a string of juicy sausages for his breakfast. There he sat, holding the pan over the fire, and as the sausage was sizzling and frizzling in the pan, Fritzl was lost in pleasant thoughts.

"A mug of cider now," that's what he was thinking. "A mug of apple cider with my sausage—that would be just the thing."

No sooner thought than done.

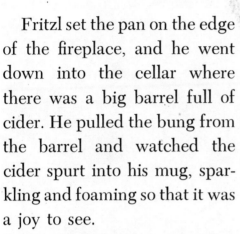

Fritzl set the pan on the edge of the fireplace, and he went down into the cellar where there was a big barrel full of cider. He pulled the bung from the barrel and watched the cider spurt into his mug, sparkling and foaming so that it was a joy to see.

But Hulla! What was that noise up in the kitchen—such a scuffle and clatter! Could it be that Spitz-dog after the sausages? Yes, that's what it was, and when Fritzl reached the top of the stairs, there he was, that dog, dashing out of the kitchen door with the string of juicy sausages flying after him.

Fritzl made for him, crying, "Hulla! Hulla! Hey, hi, ho, hulla!" But the dog wouldn't stop. Fritzl ran, Spitz ran too. Fritzl ran fast, Spitz ran faster, and the end of it was that the dog got away and our Fritzl had to give up the chase.

"Na, na! What's gone is gone," said Fritzl, shrugging his shoulders. And so he turned back, puffing and panting, and mopping his face with his big red handkerchief.

But the cider, now! Had he put the bung back in the barrel? No, that he hadn't, for he was still holding the bung in his fist.

With big fast steps Fritzl hurried home, but it was too late, for look! The cider had filled the mug and had run all over the cellar besides.

Fritzl looked at the cellar full of cider. Then he scratched his head and said, "Na, na! What's gone is gone."

Well, now it was high time to churn the butter. Fritzl filled the churn with good rich cream, took it under a tree and began to churn with all his might. His little Kinndli was out there too, playing Moo-cow among the daisies. The sky was blue, the sun right gay and golden, and the flowers, they were like angels' eyes blinking in the grass.

"This is pleasant now," thought Fritzl, as he churned away. "At last I can rest my weary legs. But wait! What about the cow? I've forgotten all about her and she hasn't had a drop of water all morning, poor thing."

With big fast steps Fritzl ran to the barn, carrying a bucket of cool fresh water for the cow. And high time it was, I can tell you, for the poor creature's tongue was hanging out of her mouth with the long thirst that was in her. She was hungry too, as a man could well see by the looks of her, so Fritzl took her from the barn and started off with her to the green grassy meadow.

But wait! There was that Kinndli to think of—she would surely get into trouble if he went out to the meadow. No, better not take the cow to the meadow at all. Better keep her nearby on the roof. The roof? Yes, the roof!

Fritzl's house was not covered with shingles or tin or tile—it was covered with moss and sod, and a fine crop of grass and flowers grew there.

To take the cow up on the roof was not so hard as you might think, either. Fritzl's house was built into the side of a hill. Up the little hill, over a little shed, and from there to the green grassy roof. That was all there was to do and it was soon done.

The cow liked it right well up there on the roof and was soon munching away with a will, so Fritzl hurried back to his churning.

But Hulla! Hui! What did he see there under the tree? Kinndli was climbing up the churn—the churn was tipping! spilling! falling! and now, there on the grass lay Kinndli, all covered with half-churned cream and butter.

"So that's the end of our butter," said Fritzl, and blinked and blinked his blue eyes. Then he shrugged his shoulders and said, "Na, na! What's gone is gone."

He picked up his dripping Kinndli and set her in the sun to dry. But the sun, now! It had climbed high up into the heavens. Noontime it was, no dinner made, and Liesi would soon be home for a bite to eat.

With big fast steps Fritzl hurried off to the garden. He gathered potatoes and onions, carrots and cabbages, beets and beans, turnips, parsley and celery.

"A little of everything, that will make a good soup," said Fritzl as he went back to the house, his arms so full of vegetables that he could not even close the garden gate behind him.

He sat on a bench in the kitchen and began cutting and paring away. How the man did work, and how the peelings and parings did fly!

But now there was a great noise above him. Fritzl jumped to his feet.

"That cow," he said, "she's sliding around right much up there on the roof. She might slip off and break her neck."

Up on the roof went Fritzl once more, this time with loops of heavy rope. Now listen carefully, and I will tell you what he did with it. He took one end of the rope and tied it around the cow's middle. The other end of the rope he dropped down the chimney and this he pulled through the fireplace in the kitchen below.

And then? And then he took the end of the rope which was hanging out of the fireplace and tied it around his own middle with a good tight knot. That's what he did.

"Oh, yo! Oh ho!" he chuckled. "That will keep the cow from falling off the roof." And he began to whistle as he went on with his work.

He heaped some sticks on the fireplace and set a big kettle of water over it.

"Na, na!" he said. "Things are going as they should at last, and we'll soon have a good big soup! Now I'll put the vegetables in the kettle—"

And that he did.

"And now I'll put in the bacon—"

And that he did too.

"And now I'll light the fire—"

But that he never did, for just then, with a bump and a thump, the cow slipped over the edge of the roof after all; and our Fritzl—well, he was whisked up into the chimney and there he dangled, poor man, and couldn't get up and couldn't get down.

Before long, there came Liesi home from the fields with the water jug in her hand and the scythe over her shoulder.

But Hulla! Hui! What was that hanging over the edge of the roof? The cow? Yes, the cow, and half-choked she was, too, with her eyes bulging and her tongue hanging out.

Hulla! Hui!

G. Armstrong

Liesi lost no time. She took her scythe—and ritsch! rotsch!
—the rope was cut, and there was the cow wobbling on her
four legs, but alive and well, heaven be praised!

Now Liesi saw the garden with its gate wide open. There
were the pigs and the goats and all the geese too. They were
full to bursting, but the garden, alas! was empty.

Liesi walked on, and now what did she see? The churn
up-turned, and Kinndli there in the sun, stiff and sticky with
dried cream and butter.

Liesi hurried on. There was Spitz-dog on the grass. He was
full of sausages and looked none too well.

Liesi looked at the cellar. There was the cider all over the
floor and halfway up the stairs besides.

Liesi looked in the kitchen. The floor! It was piled high
with peelings and parings, and littered with dishes and pans.

At last Liesi saw the fireplace. Hu! Hulla! Hui! What was
that in the soup-kettle? Two arms were waving, two legs were
kicking, and a gurgle, bubbly and weak-like, was coming up
out of the water.

"Na, na! What can this mean?" cried Liesi. She did not know
(but we do—yes?) that when she saved the cow outside, something happened to Fritzl. Yes, as soon as the cow's rope was
cut, Fritzl, poor man, he dropped down the chimney and crash!
splash! fell right into the kettle of soup in the fireplace.

Liesi lost no time. She pulled at the two arms and tugged at the legs—and there, dripping and spluttering, with a cabbage-leaf in his hair, celery in his pocket, and a sprig of parsley over one ear, was her Fritzl.

"Na, na, my man!" said Liesi. "Is that the way you keep house—yes?"

"Oh Liesi, Liesi!" sputtered Fritzl. "You're right—that work of yours, 'tis none too easy."

"'Tis a little hard at first," said Liesi, "but tomorrow, maybe, you'll do better."

"Nay, nay!" cried Fritzl. "What's gone is gone, and so is my housework from this day on. Please, please, my Liesi—let me go back to my work in the fields, and never more will I say that my work is harder than yours."

"Well then," said Liesi, "if that's how it is, we surely can live in peace and happiness for ever and ever."

And that they did.

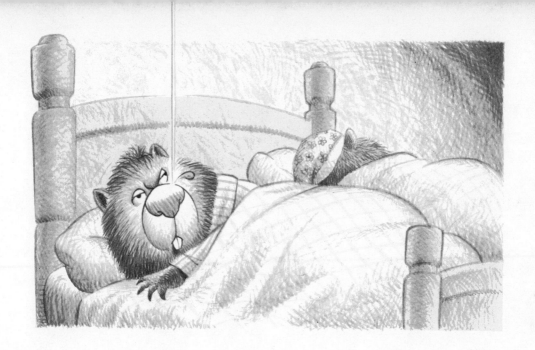

Mr. Groundhog
Turns Around

by James T. Brady

illustrated by Donald G. Wheeler

A drop of icy water fell right on Mr. Groundhog's nose. His nose twitched, but he went on sleeping. Plop! Another drop landed in the same place. This time Mr. Groundhog opened his eyes. At first he couldn't remember where he was, he had been sleeping so long and so soundly. But then he recognized the inside of his home, and he reached over to where his wife was snoring peacefully. "Time to wake up!" he called as he shook her. "Wake up!"

Mrs. Groundhog raised her head just a little. "What's the matter?"

"Spring's the matter, that's what!" declared Mr. Groundhog. "Look at the water coming into our house!"

Mrs. Groundhog sat up and looked around. Sure enough, big drops of water were coming through the roof and dripping down on the floor. At sight of this, Mrs. Groundhog woke up completely, jumped out of bed, scurried for her maple-leaf mop, and went to work mopping up the puddles.

"The snow must be melting outside," Mr. Groundhog said.

"Maybe you're right," his wife admitted. "What day is it, anyway?"

Mr. Groundhog waddled over to the groundhog calendar, his tail trailing behind him. "It must be February second," he announced. "We've been asleep since November. I'm tired of being indoors so long."

"I'll bet it's still cold outside, though," Mrs. Groundhog said.

"Nonsense!" answered her husband. "You can see the sunlight shining at the door." Mr. Groundhog pointed down one of the passages leading to the outdoors. "Besides," he added, patting his stomach with a furry paw, "I'm starved. I could eat a whole field of nice red clover."

"Don't get too excited about food," warned Mrs. Groundhog. "It's probably too early in the year to find anything to eat."

Mr. Groundhog didn't answer. He was already halfway down the tunnel where he saw the sunlight. As he came closer to the entrance, the air was much colder. He shivered a little and said to himself,

"It *is* a bit chilly!" But then he thought of the sweet red clover which might be waiting for him in the fields outside.

He hurried on. When he reached the outside, an icy blast nipped his nose, but he said stubbornly, "Ah, this fresh air smells good. Spring is here!"

He put his head out of the hole, then one paw and then another, until he was completely out of the tunnel. There was plenty of sunshine, to be sure, but the air was cold, and Mr. Groundhog's paws were freezing on the hard snow underfoot. He couldn't see a sign of clover, or, for that matter, of anything green. He faced the sun, and this warmed his nose but did not reach his tail, which felt very, very cold. "I'd better turn around," he remarked to himself, and turned his back to the sun. He waved his tail to and fro, searching the ground for just one little bit of green grass.

Then suddenly he saw something close to him that made every hair on his body stand on end! Quick as lightning Mr. Groundhog scampered back into his hole.

"My goodness!" exclaimed Mrs. Groundhog. "Whatever is the matter with you?"

But Mr. Groundhog was so frightened that when he opened his mouth to answer her, not a sound came out.

"Was it a fox?" asked Mrs. Groundhog. "Was it a weasel?"

Still Mr. Groundhog didn't answer. He just shook his head. "Well, what was it?"

Finally Mr. Groundhog found his voice and said, "We might as well go back to sleep for a few more weeks." And so saying, he crawled into bed, curled up in a ball and went fast asleep.

"I guess I may as well have another nap myself," said Mrs. Groundhog, yawning, "But I do wonder what it could have been that frightened my husband?"

Do *you* know what it was?

What Mary Jo Shared

by Janice May Udry

illustrated by Eleanor Mill

Mary Jo never shared anything at school. She was too shy to stand before the other children and tell about anything. She didn't think they would listen to her.

Almost every day her teacher, Miss Willet, would say, "And Mary Jo, do you have something to share with us this morning?"

And Mary Jo always shook her head and looked down at the floor.

"Why don't you ever share anything?" her friend Laurie asked.

"I will some day," said Mary Jo. "I just don't want to yet."

Mary Jo really did want to share, but she was afraid to try.

Almost every evening when he came home, Mary Jo's father asked, "Did you share something at school today, Mary Jo?"

"Not yet," she always answered.

One morning it was raining hard.

"I'll share my new umbrella," thought Mary Jo as soon as she woke up and saw the rain pouring down the window. She could hardly wait. She hurried with breakfast and hurried with dressing.

Finally it was time to put on her new pink raincoat and take her own pink umbrella to school.

This was the first umbrella Mary Jo had ever owned. Before, when it rained, she walked under her sister's umbrella.

Mary Jo had picked this one out herself in the store.

On the handle was a chain and tag. Mary Jo had written her name, the name of the school, and "Room 101" on the tag herself.

She hurried up the hill from the car, holding her umbrella against the heavy rain.

At the door she shook her umbrella and then carried it in, dripping along the hall.

When she got to the door of her room, she saw a whole row of umbrellas drying in the hall! They were all sizes and colors. Some of the other umbrellas even had tags on the handles like Mary Jo's.

180

"Almost everybody in my room has an umbrella, too,"
thought Mary Jo. "I guess that isn't a good thing to share after
all."

So when Miss Willet said, "And Mary Jo, do you have something to share with us this morning?" Mary Jo shook her head
and looked at the floor.

The next week Mary Jo and her brother caught a grasshopper and put it in a jar with holes punched on the top so
it could breathe.

"I'll share the grasshopper!" thought Mary Jo.

She wrapped the jar carefully in a cloth and put it in a
brown paper bag. That way, even if she dropped the jar, it
wouldn't break.

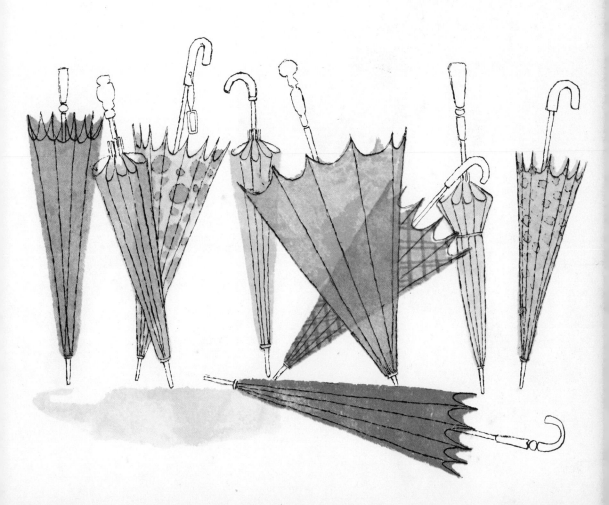

She hurried to school carrying the wrapped jar carefully under one arm and her lunch box in the other hand.

When she came to the door of her room, several children were clustered around a boy named Jimmy. They were all looking at something he had brought in a jar.

Mary Jo put her lunch box and sack carefully on the shelf. She hung up her sweater. Then she went to see what the other children were looking at.

"Jimmy's got *six* grasshoppers in a jar!" said Laurie. "He caught all of them himself."

Mary Jo thought about her one grasshopper—and how her brother had helped her catch it.

"I guess I won't share my grasshopper after all," thought Mary Jo.

So when Miss Willet said, "And Mary Jo, do you have something to share with us this morning?" Mary Jo shook her head and looked at the floor.

All the other children in Miss Willet's room shared things. They shared letters from their aunts, or they shared their pets—turtles,

white mice,

rabbits,

and kittens.

They shared things they found at the beach and things they found in the woods.

Mary Jo didn't have an aunt to get letters from, she didn't have any pets, and she never found anything at the beach or in the woods that someone else hadn't already shared.

But Mary Jo finally became determined to share something that no one else had shared. It got so she could hardly think of anything else.

One night Mary Jo even dreamed that she wanted to share her new pet elephant.

But when she brought him to Miss Willet's room, he was too big to squeeze through the door, no matter how hard she shoved!

So—in her dream—she sadly led her new pet away.

"What shall I share?" she pondered over and over.

Her father came home.

"Did you share something at school today, Mary Jo?" he asked her as usual.

And as usual, Mary Jo said, "Not yet."

Then, suddenly, Mary Jo thought of something!

"Could you go to school with me tomorrow for a little while?" she asked her father.

"Tomorrow? Yes," said her father. "I don't have a class until eleven o'clock."

Mary Jo's father was a
teacher in the high school.

"Good!" said Mary Jo. "Then
you can come and hear me
share something."

"All right," said her father.
"I'll be there! What are you
going to share?"

"Wait and see," said Mary Jo.

As soon as Mary Jo and her father got to school the next morning, Mary Jo introduced her father to Miss Willet.

Miss Willet said that they were very glad to have him visit their class.

"I've got something to share today," said Mary Jo.

"Fine," said Miss Willet. "There is the bell."

Mary Jo's father sat by the window in one of the guest chairs while the

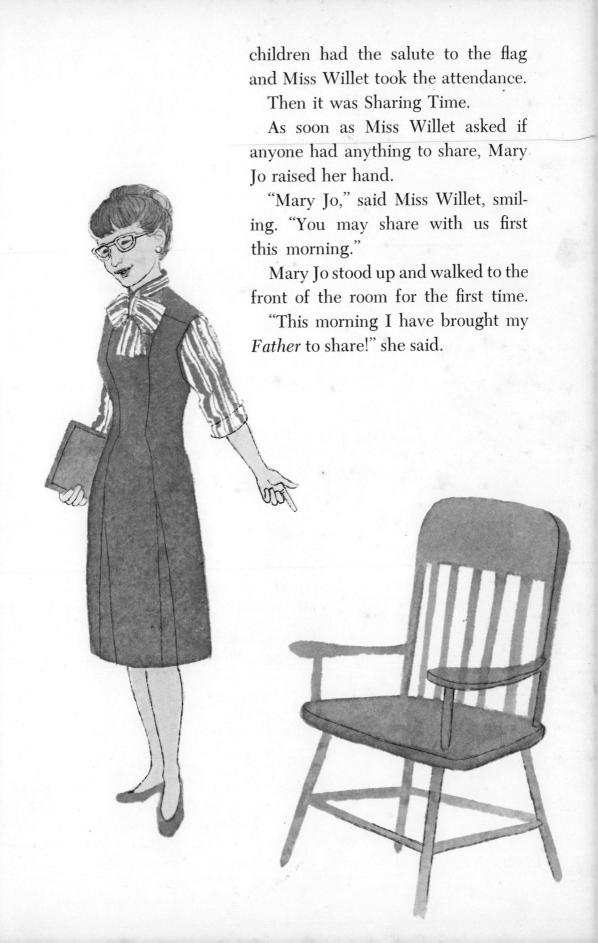

children had the salute to the flag and Miss Willet took the attendance.

Then it was Sharing Time.

As soon as Miss Willet asked if anyone had anything to share, Mary Jo raised her hand.

"Mary Jo," said Miss Willet, smiling. "You may share with us first this morning."

Mary Jo stood up and walked to the front of the room for the first time.

"This morning I have brought my *Father* to share!" she said.

In spite of herself she giggled a little. This made all the children smile, and they turned to look at Mary Jo's father.

He didn't mind at all.

He stood, bowed his head a little in his friendly way, and sat down again, waiting to be shared.

"This is my father, Mr. William Wood. He is thirty-six years old and has a wife and three children. His youngest child is me," said Mary Jo.

Jimmy raised his hand.

"My father was born in Montana,"
said Jimmy. "Where was your father
born?"

"He was born in California," said
Mary Jo. "My father teaches English
in high school. He likes to read a
lot. He writes quite a bit, too."

She took a deep breath and went on.

"He is a good swimmer and knows
how to sail boats. He likes to go
fishing and hiking."

"So does my father!" said Laurie.

"My father builds houses," said
another child.

191

"My father travels all over the country," said another child.

They *all* wanted to share their fathers, it seemed.

"Children," said Miss Willet, "it is Mary Jo who is sharing her father today. Please be a little more quiet."

"Before my father grew up, he was a little boy," said Mary Jo. Then her face turned hot because that sounded sort of silly.

All the children laughed.

But Mary Jo went on.

"Sometimes he wasn't too well behaved," said Mary Jo.

"What did he do?" asked one of the boys.

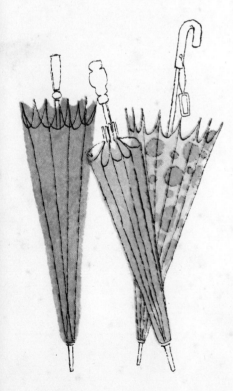

"Well, once he locked his little brother out of the house . . . and once he ate a whole chocolate cake that his mother was saving for an afternoon club meeting," said Mary Jo. "And now, my father will say a few words."

Mr. Wood stood and smiled and made a little speech about how he had enjoyed visiting Miss Willet's class.

The children clapped, and Mary Jo and her father sat down.

Mary Jo felt good. At last she had shared something that no one else had thought of sharing.